REVELATION

by Donnie V. Rader

2017 One Stone Press.
All rights reserved. No part of this book may be reproduced
in any form without written permission of the publisher.

Published by:
One Stone Press
979 Lovers Lane
Bowling Green, KY 42103

Printed in the United States of America

ISBN (10 Digit): 1-941422-21-7
ISBN (13 Digit): 978-1-941422-21-2

We want to thank Manna Maps for allowing the use of their map. These maps
can be purchased and downloaded from
www.biblemaps.com.

Supplemental Materials Available:
PowerPoint slides for each lesson
Answer key
Downloadable PDF

1.800.428.0121
www.onestone.com

Table of Contents

Lesson 1	Introduction to the Book of Revelation	5
Lesson 2	Rev. 1: John's Vision of Christ Commissioning Him to Write	15
Lesson 3	Rev. 2:1-7: Letter to the Church at Ephesus	21
Lesson 4	Rev. 2:8-11: Letter to the Church at Smyrna	27
Lesson 5	Rev. 2:12-17: Letter to the Church at Pergamos	31
Lesson 6	Rev. 2:18-29: Letter to the Church at Thyatira	37
Lesson 7	Rev. 3:1-6: Letter to the Church at Sardis	43
Lesson 8	Rev. 3:7-13: Letter to the Church at Philadelphia	47
Lesson 9	Rev. 3:14-22: Letter to the Church at Laodicea	51
Lesson 10	Rev. 4 and 5: The Throne Scene	57
Lesson 11	Rev. 6: Opening of the Six Seals	65
Lesson 12	Rev. 7: An Interlude: The Sealing of God's People	71
Lesson 13	Rev. 8: Opening the Seventh Seal: Four of the Seven Trumpets	75
Lesson 14	Rev. 9: Fifth and Sixth Trumpets	81
Lesson 15	Rev. 10: An Interlude: The Angel and the Little Book	87
Lesson 16	Rev. 11: Measuring the Temple, Two Witnesses, and the Seventh Trumpet	91
Lesson 17	Rev. 12: The Woman and the Dragon at War	97
Lesson 18	Rev. 13: The Two Beasts	103
Lesson 19	Rev. 14: The Victorious Lamb	109
Lesson 20	Rev. 15 and 16: Seven Bowls of Wrath	115
Lesson 21	Rev. 17: The Great Harlot	123
Lesson 22	Rev. 18: The Fall of Babylon the Harlot	127
Lesson 23	Rev. 19: Victory Over the Harlot and the Beast	133
Lesson 24	Rev. 20: Victory Over Satan and The Final Judgment	139
Lesson 25	Rev. 21: Victory in Heaven	145
Lesson 26	Rev. 22: Warnings About the Book	151

Introduction to the Book of Revelation

A study of any book of the Bible, especially the book of Revelation, needs a proper introduction to do it justice. Getting the principles down that are dealt with in this first lesson, not only makes all the difference in understanding the book, but makes the difference in whether you enjoy and appreciate this study.

Can it be Understood?

Some dismiss the book before attempting to study it. In some churches, when they get to this book, they skip it and jump back to Matthew because they think it cannot be understood.

There are extreme attitudes and approaches to the book. On the one hand, some think the book is meaningless. Martin Luther "at one time refused to have the book in his canon because, in his opinion, it was impossible to understand it."[1] On the other hand, some seek to prove anything they dream up by a manipulation of the symbolic language. No doubt, the book holds a certain attraction to those who are interested in the mysterious.

We must approach this study with the admission that there are difficulties. However, one can clearly understand the main thrust of the book.

The Nature of the Book

It is the apocalypse. The writer identifies this book as "The Revelation of Jesus Christ" (1:1). The term "Revelation" is from the word *apokalupsis* (apocalypse). The word means "an uncovering, laying bare, making naked."[2] Thus, the book uncovers through symbols, imagery and visions impending persecutions and victory of the saints. Both words (revelation and apocalypse) suggest an understanding.

Other apocalyptic literature. Other such books include Daniel, Ezekiel (both written in Babylonian captivity) and Zechariah (written during the Persian rule). Parts of Isaiah and Joel fit this mold as well. Jesus' discussion of the destruction of Jerusalem (Matt. 24, Mark 13, Luke 21) is the only other apocalyptic literature in the New Testament besides Revelation.

The conditions out of which apocalyptic literature grew. Trials, suffering and adversity are the backdrop of the afore mentioned books. "It is essentially a literature of the oppressed who saw no hope for the nation simply in terms of politics or on the plane of human history."[3] This type of writing pictures the present great suffering in contrast to a glorious future.

---

1 Ray Summers, *Worthy Is the Lamb*, xiv.
2 Joseph Henry Thayer, *A Greek-English Lexicon of the New Testament*, 62.
3 D. S. Russell as quoted by Ferrell Jenkins, *The Old Testament in the Book of Revelation*, 35.

Characteristics of Apocalyptic Literature. While more could be listed, we present four here.

1. *Imagery.* One of the main characteristics of apocalyptic literature is the use of symbols and signs. The author tells us in the first verse that this message is "signified" (1:1).[4] Some of the symbolic terms will be understood in light of the Old Testament. Some will be explained in the context (i.e. 1:20).

2. *Visions.* This method was used by prophets as well, but is particularly used in apocalyptic material. "These visions vary from scenes in heaven to scenes on earth."[5]

3. *Predictive element.* In the midst of the darkness of suffering, the future triumph, vindication and relief are presented.

4. *Dramatic effect.* This helps the reader to vividly see the point. Details that are given for the dramatic effect should not be pressed too far.

Why write in this form using symbolism? Why is there a need for apocalyptic literature? Why couldn't the writer forget the symbolic and state the facts in simple terms? Using this method, it is easy to instruct and encourage God's people without playing into the hands of the enemy (in this book it is the Roman authorities). There would be a danger to the writer and the recipients if the message was clearly understood by the oppressor. This method conceals and at the same time reveals. "While instructing and encouraging His saints, God was concealing His purpose from the gross and hardhearted unbelievers. God's choice of method in doing this was prudent and brilliant."[6]

To illustrate, I read a report of some brethren laboring in a country that forbade them to assemble, worship and make converts. Their mail and phone calls were perhaps being monitored. So, in communicating to family and brethren back in the States they would say, "We ate more bread today" referring to assembling for the Lord's supper. If someone was baptized, they would say that another "went swimming today." The message goes through without the enemy understanding.

A warning! It is very easy to let this type of literature become the foundation of fallacious interpretations.

Methods of Interpretation

The method one uses to approach the book of Revelation makes all the difference in the outcome of his interpretation. As one studies, perhaps using several commentaries, he must be aware they may differ greatly because they are using different methods. Here is a brief summary of the different methods.[7]

---

4   The word means "'to give a sign, indicate' (*sema*, 'a sign': cf. SIGN, No. 1), 'to signify,' is so translated in John 12:33; 18:32; 21:19; Acts 11:28; 25:27; Rev. 1:1, where perhaps the suggestion is that of expressing by signs" (W. E. Vine, *Vine's Complete Expository Dictionary of Old and New Testament Words*, 2:575).
5   Summers, *ibid.*, 18.
6   Homer Hailey, *Revelation, An Introduction and Commentary*, 18.
7   Ray Summers devotes a whole chapter to a discussion of these methods (*ibid.*, 27-51). Here is a summary of what Summers presents.

The futurist method. This approach says the book deals with events at the end of the world. It claims Revelation is a book of unfulfilled prophecy. Everything in the book closely relates to the second coming of Christ. Those who hold this view think chapters 4-19 deal with the period of seven years of tribulation.[8] This method takes most of the book literally.

There are at least three problems with this method. (1) The things in Revelation were to shortly come to pass (1:1, 3; 22:6, 10). (2) This method would make the message meaningless to those who were addressed. Summers was correct when he said, "I do not believe that any interpretation of Revelation can be correct if it was meaningless and if it failed to bring practical help and comfort to those who first received the book."[9] (3) It is based on the erroneous doctrine of Premillennialism.

The continuous – historical method. This method views the book as a forecast of the history of the church, i.e. a prophecy of the apostasy and formation of the Catholic church.[10] The problem with this approach, like the one before, is that it is meaningless to those who received the book. Additionally, it is based on a lot of assumption.

The philosophy of history method. This method says the book discusses the forces of good and evil which underlie the events rather than the events themselves. This view looks at the book as setting forth the principles of how God deals with all men in all ages. For example, the beast of the sea (chapter 13) is simply the secular powers that are opposed to the truth. John is viewed as the giver of truth.

This approach places the point of the book too far removed from the situation of those to whom the book is directed. Furthermore, it ignores the historical setting.

The preterist method. "Preter" means past or beyond. Thus, this method views the events of the book as already taken place in the past. All has been fulfilled in the days of the Roman empire.

This view has some merit. It frames the book in the historical background, thus, making it meaningful to those to whom it was intended. The objection we offer is that it only applies the book to the events under the Roman empire and does not allow for spiritual application for successive generations.

The historical-background method. This approach takes part of the preterist view and combines it with the philosophy of history method. This makes the book meaningful to those to whom it was addressed. It keeps in mind the figurative language. It puts the book in the social, political and religious setting of the day. However, it seeks to grasp the meaning of the visions as a whole without pressing the details. This method recognizes that there are some things in the book yet to be fulfilled (i.e. the final judgment of chapters 20-22). The principles found in the book (i.e. God is still on his throne and in control – chapter 4) apply beyond the days of the Roman Emperors.

This is the view that will be followed in this study.[11]

---

8   This is part of the Premillennial doctrine.
9   *Ibid*, vii.
10 Albert Barnes, among others, take this view.
11 Homer Hailey, *ibid.*, Robert Harkrider, *Revelation*, and Ray Summers, *ibid.* follow this method in their commentaries.

The Old Testament in the Book of Revelation

"The book of Revelation is the work of a Jew saturated with Old Testament prophecy."[12] Much of the book will be missed if one doesn't have at least some understanding of the Old Testament.

The book is rich in Old Testament phraseology.[13] Westcott and Hort suggest there are over 400 references to the Old Testament in the Revelation. H. B. Swete says 278 verses (of the 404) in Revelation contain references to the Jewish Scripture. However, there is not one direct quotation from the Old Testament. John never says he is quoting the Old Testament. Merrill C. Tenny says that the significant number of allusions to the Old Testament are 348. Of that number, 95 are repeated, leaving 250. That is an average of more than 10 per chapter.

Why is the book filled with so many Old Testament allusions? We suggest three reasons:

1. The readers would recognize the allusions and sources referred to while the oppressor would not.

2. Apocalyptic literature demands figures which are found in the Old Testament.

3. The circumstances of this book are somewhat parallel to those in the Old Testament. Exodus deals with God's judgment upon Egypt. Daniel and Ezekiel were in exile and oppressed. The message of God ruling in the kingdoms of men (Dan. 4:25) is certainly found in the Revelation. Ezekiel, Daniel, and Jeremiah dealt with the overthrow of literal Babylon. In Revelation, Babylon (Rome) will be overthrown.

The Date of the Book

The dating of the book is one of the most debated points in a study of Revelation. All agree that there is widespread severe persecution at the hand of a Roman Emperor. Some think it is Nero (64-68 AD), thus putting the writing of the book before the destruction of Jerusalem (70 AD).[14] Others believe (including this writer) the Emperor to be Domitian (81-96 AD). Foy E. Wallace and Art Ogden argue for the early date in their commentaries. Homer Hailey, Ray Summers, Robert Harkrider, and Wayne Jackson argue for the later date in their works.

The circumstances do not fit the time of Nero. Concerning Nero, Homer Hailey observed, "There is no solid evidence that Nero's persecution extended beyond the city of Rome itself... From available evidence, it appears that Nero's persecution was not aimed at the annihilation of Christianity, that it did not extend beyond Rome and that he issued no formal edict against the Christians."[15] Hailey further argues that while Nero accepted worship, he was restrained with reference to being deified until after he was dead. However, "Domitian avidly courted worship of himself by the people and wanted them to look upon him as a god."[16] Ray Summers makes the same point. "Revelation clearly indicates that the Christians were being persecuted because they refused to worship the emperor. There is no such demand

---
12 Ferrell Jenkins, *The Old Testament in the Book of Revelation*, 21.
13 The points or statistics listed in this section are a summary from Jenkins, *ibid.*, 23.
14 Those who argue this believe they see evidence in Revelation 11 that the temple is still standing.
15 *Ibid.*, 29-30.
16 *Ibid.*, 31.

during the time of Nero…The Neronian persecution was confined to Rome; it never reached the other parts of the empire."[17]

External evidence that Revelation fits the time of Domitian's reign. "Irenaeus (A.D. 180), a student of Polycarp (who was a disciple of the apostle John), wrote that the apocalyptic vision 'was seen not very long ago, almost in our own generation, at the close of the reign of Domitian' (*Against Heresies* 30). The testimony of Irenaeus, not far removed from the apostolic age, is first rate. He places the book near the end of Domitian's reign, and that ruler died in A.D. 96. Irenaeus seems to be unaware of any other view for the date of the book of Revelation."[18]

"Clement of Alexandria (A.D. 155-215) says that John returned from the isle of Patmos 'after the tyrant was dead' (*Who Is the Rich Man?* 42), and Eusebius, known as the 'Father of Church History,' identifies the 'tyrant' as Domitian (*Ecclesiastical History* III.23)."[19]

Internal evidence that Revelation fits the time of Domitian's reign. The letter to the church at Ephesus (2:1-7) shows a dramatic change in the church from what we see at the time Paul wrote Ephesians (60-64 AD). It is not likely that such a change would have developed in ten years or less. The letter to Laodicea (3:14-22) had nothing to commend in the church. Yet, when Paul wrote to the Colossians (62 AD), he indicates that they were commendable (Col. 4:13). It doesn't seem likely that such a change could take place in less than ten years.

"Then consider this fact. The church at Laodicea is represented as existing under conditions of great wealth. She was rich and had need of nothing (3:17). In A.D. 60, though, Laodicea had been almost entirely destroyed by an earthquake. Surely it would have required more than eight or nine years for that city to have risen again to the state of affluence described in Revelation."[20]

Thus, we put the date about 95-96 AD near the end of Domitian's reign.[21]

The Author

The text says it was John (Rev. 1:1, 4, 9; 22:8).

Early writers attribute it to John. Justin Martyer (100-165 AD), Irenaeus (120-202 AD), Clement of Alexandria (153-217 AD), Tertullian (145-220 AD), and Origen (185-254 AD) credit John the apostle as the author of Revelation.

Some facts about John. John was a son of Zebedee and Salome (Matt. 27:56; Mark 15:40-41). Some infer from John 19:25 that Salome and Mary (mother of Jesus) were sisters, thus

---

17 *Ibid.*, 80.
18 Wayne Jackson, "When Was the Book of Revelation Written?" *ChristianCourier.com.* Access date: December 29, 2015. https://www.christiancourier.com/articles/1552-when-was-the-book-of-revelation-written.
19 Jackson, *ibid.*
20 Jackson, *ibid.*
21 For an excellent exchange on evidence for Domitian persecution see *Did Domitian Persecute Christians – An Investigation* by Ferrell Jenkins and Arthur M. Ogden (http://bibleworld.com/domper.pdf).

making Jesus and John cousins. Others dispute that. He was one of the only three at the raising of the Jairus' daughter (Mark 5:37; Luke 8:51), the transfiguration (Matt. 17:1-13), and at Gethsemane (Matt. 26:36-45).

He was very close to the Lord himself. He was the disciple Jesus loved (John 21:20). He was at Jesus' bosom at the supper (John 13:23; 21:20ff). It was John to whom he committed his mother's care (John 19:25-27).

John wrote five New Testament books: the gospel that bears his name, the three epistles that bear his name, and Revelation.

Where it was Written

John said he was on the island of Patmos (1:9). The rocky island was located about 60-70 miles south west of Ephesus and 24 miles west of Asia Minor. It was about 10 miles long and 6 miles across.

John was there "for the word of God" (1:9). He was banished to the island because of the persecution under Domitian. After the emperor's death, he returned to Ephesus. Some argue that it was written after he returned to Ephesus. This is because he said he "was" on Patmos (1:9). The encouragement to endure found within the book would seem to be of little value after the storm was over.

To Whom was it Written?

The book is addressed to the seven churches of Asia (1:4, 10, 11). Those seven are identified in chapters 2-3: Ephesus, Smyrna, Pergamos, Thyatira, Sardis, Philadelphia, and Laodicea.

It was not restricted to those seven. There were other churches in Asia such as Troas (Acts 20:7), Colossae (Col. 1:2), and Hierapolis (Col. 4:13) that surely faced the same trials at the hand of Domitian that the seven churches did. Perhaps the seven stand for all the churches that faced the same pressure.

Christians in all ages benefit from the book. While not addressed to us, surely we are included in "he who reads and those who hear" (1:3) and "everyone who hears the words of the prophecy of this book" (22:18).

Background and Circumstance

Severe persecution at the hand of Domitian was well under way at the time John wrote (1:9; 2:10, 13, 22; 3:10). Rome felt that Christianity was a threat to the government and therefore thought it best to destroy Christians.

Caesar worship was at the heart of the problem for the Christians. The Romans knew little or nothing about the one true God. For most citizens, Caesar worship was not a big problem. If other gods were already served, why not add one more? To Domitian it was a political question (loyalty to Rome). To the Christian it was a religious question (loyalty to God). William Barclay describes the dilemma.

By the time the Revelation was written Caesar worship was the one religion which covered the whole Roman Empire; and it was because of their refusal to conform to its demands that Christians were persecuted and killed. The essence of Caesar worship was that the reigning Roman Emperor, as embodying the spirit of Rome, was divine. Once a year everyone in the Empire had to appear before the magistrates in order to burn a pinch of incense to the godhead of Caesar, and to say: "Caesar is Lord." After he had done that, a man might go away and worship any god or goddess he liked, so long as that worship did not infringe decency and good order; but first of all he must go through the ceremony in which he acknowledged the Emperor as a god. The reason for all this was very simple. Rome had a vast heterogeneous empire, stretching from one end of the known world to another. It had in it many tongues, many races, many traditions, many countries. The problem was how to weld this varied mass into a self-conscious unity. There is no unifying force like the force of a common religion. None of the national religions, and none of the local gods, could conceivably have become universal. But Caesar worship could. It was the one common act and common belief which turned the Empire into a unity. And to refuse to burn the pinch of incense, and to refuse to say: "Caesar is Lord," was not an act of irreligion; it was an act of political disloyalty. If a man refused to go through the annual ceremony, the Romans did not regard him as an irreligious man; they regarded him as a bad and disaffected citizen who refused to acknowledge the greatness of Caesar and the divinity of Rome. That is why the Romans dealt with the utmost severity with the man who would not say: "Caesar is Lord." And no Christian could be persuaded to give the title Lord to anyone other than Jesus Christ. For the Christian—it was the center and essence of his creed—Jesus Christ, and Jesus Christ alone is Lord.

But we must see how this Caesar worship developed, and how it was at its peak in the time when the Revelation was written.[22]

The Message

This great book was written to encourage those Christians who were suffering persecution at the hands of the wicked Domitian. The message is that of victory of Christ and his saints over the forces of Satan. Christ will be victorious (1:18; 6:2; 11:15; 14:1; 19:16). The saints will overcome. They will endure (13:10; 14:12), have their robes washed (7:14; 22:14 ASV), have victory over the beast (15:2), and come out of the tribulation (7:14).

"The book is designed to encourage Christians to be faithful in the face of all opposition and persecution, regardless of how terrible the onslaught might be."[23]

A summary verse for the book might be Revelation 17:14, "These will make war with the Lamb, and the Lamb will overcome them, for He is Lord of lords and King of kings; and those *who are* with Him *are* called, chosen, and faithful."

---

22 *The Revelation of John*, 1:19-20.
23 Hailey, *ibid.*, 52.

The Significance of Numbers

The reader of Revelation must be aware of how numbers are used. The symbolic significance of the numbers "must be determined by the use made of the object considered. It is from the use made of numerical figures that we are to determine any symbolic significance. This may not be totally satisfactory, because it appears inconclusive, but to this writer there is no alternative."[24] The symbolic use of numbers is necessary in this type of literature.

The following numbers are used in a symbolic sense in Revelation.[25]

One – unity.

Two – strength.

Three – divine (i.e. Father, Son and Holy Spirit).

Four – world, creation (i.e. "four corners of the earth" 17:1; 20:8).

Six – short of seven, thus failure.

Seven – completeness, totality. (i.e. seven seals 5:1; seven bowls of wrath 15:7; etc.).

Ten – power or fullness.

Twelve – religious number (i.e. twelve tribes, twelve apostles).

Three and a half (times, time and half a time 12:14) – broken seven, thus incomplete – an indefinite period.

---

24 Hailey, *ibid.*, 41.
25 For a more thorough discussion of the significance of numbers see Homer Hailey, *ibid.*, 41-48.

An Outline of the Book[26]

I. Struggle on Earth (1-11)

    A. *John's Vision (1)*
    B. *Letters to 7 churches (2-3)*
    C. *God in control (4-5)*
    D. *Opening of seven seals (6-11)*

II. Christ And The Dragon In Conflict (12-22)
(Deeper Spiritual Meaning)

    A. *War (12-14)*
    B. *Bowls of Wrath (15-16)*
    C. *Fall of Babylon the Harlot (17-18)*
    D. *Victory of God's people (19-21)*
    E. *Warnings about the Book (22)*

Points to Remember as We Study Revelation

1. The letter was understood by those to whom it was sent. Thus, it can be understood today.

2. There was a need for using symbolic language.

3. Speculative guessing is dangerous.

4. Interpretations must agree with the context of the book and the rest of the Bible.

5. We cannot afford to be dogmatic.

Questions

1. What does *apokalupsis* (apocalypse) mean? _____
   _____

2. What other books are apocalyptic in nature? _____
   _____

3. Why is it necessary to write in symbolic language? _____
   _____
   _____

4. What is the futurist method of interpretation and what objections can be made against it? _____
   _____
   _____

---

26 Parts of this little outline are adapted from Robert Harkrider's outline in his workbook, *Revelation*, 8-9.

5. What is the continuous – historical method of interpretation and what objections can be made against it? _____
_____
_____

6. What method of interpretation is the proper approach? _____
_____

7. Why is the book filled with so many Old Testament allusions? _____
_____
_____

8. What evidence can be given for the date of the book to be a late date (95-96)? ___
_____
_____

9. How was Caesar worship viewed by Rome and how was it viewed by Christians? ___
_____
_____

10. What is the message of the book of Revelation? _____
_____
_____

Revelation 1
John's Vision Of Christ Commissioning Him To Write

Lesson 2

Outline

I. The Content and Nature of the Book (vv. 1-3)

A. *Revelation of Christ which God gave him (v. 1)*
B. *Things that shortly take place (vv. 1, 3)*
C. *Signified (v. 1)*

II. Salutations to the Seven Churches (vv. 4-8)

A. *Grace and peace (v. 4)*
B. *From God and his Spirit (v. 4, 8)*
C. *From Christ (vv. 5-8)*
   1. Faithful witness (v. 5)
   2. Firstborn from the dead (v. 5)
   3. Ruler over the kings of the earth (v. 5)
   4. Loved us and washed us from sin (v. 5)
   5. Made us kings and priests (v. 6)
   6. Is coming in the clouds (v. 7)

III. John's Vision of Christ (vv. 9-20)

A. *Where John was – Patmos (v. 9)*
B. *Vision of Christ (vv. 10-18)*
C. *Commission to write (vv. 11, 19)*
D. *Explanation of the vision (v. 20)*

Key Verse that Summarizes the Chapter

Revelation 1:11

Saying, "I am the Alpha and the Omega, the First and the Last," and, "What you see, write in a book and send it to the seven churches which are in Asia: to Ephesus, to Smyrna, to Pergamos, to Thyatira, to Sardis, to Philadelphia, and to Laodicea."

The book opens with an explanation of the content and nature of the book, who is sending the message, and a vision of Christ. When the oppressed Christians, to whom this book is directed, hear the reading of these 20 verses (v. 3), they are already seeing a picture of victory.

The Content and Nature of the Book (vv. 1-3)

Revelation of Christ which God gave him (v. 1). Here is the content of the book—it is the Revelation of Jesus Christ. As noted in lesson 1, the term "Revelation" is from the word *apokalupsis* (apocalypse). The word means "an uncovering, laying bare, making naked."[1] Thus, the book uncovers or makes known the impending persecutions and victory of the saints. This is not the Revelation of John, but of Christ. It is called the "testimony of Jesus Christ" (v. 2).

Things that shortly take place (vv. 1, 3)[2]. The things about which John writes (called "prophecy" v. 3) were to "shortly take place" (v. 1) for the "time is near" (v. 3). "The things revealed here must happen shortly, or the cause will be lost – Domitian will stamp out Christianity completely."[3] This gives the assurance of immediate or near fulfillment of the promise of victory "even though the book does deal with the final judgment and the new order of things beyond the judgment, which were in the distant future and are yet to come (20:11; 21:8)."[4]

A blessing is pronounced upon the one who reads (perhaps a reference to a lector who publicly reads the Scriptures, cf. Luke 4:16) and those who hear and keep the words recorded (v. 3).

Signified (v. 1). Here we learn about the nature of the book. The word translated "signified" means "'to give a sign, indicate'...Rev. 1:1, where perhaps the suggestion is that of expressing by signs."[5] Thus, the Revelation of Christ is delivered in highly symbolic language as illustrated in the vision of Christ (vv. 9-20). Summers calls the Revelation a "divine picture book."[6]

Salutations to the Seven Churches (vv. 4-8)

Grace and peace (v. 4). While this is a greeting to the seven churches, it is more. Perhaps implied is the fact that the same grace by which they were saved will see them through to victory over Rome. Peace comes as a result of grace.

From God and his Spirit (v. 4, 8). The salutation is from God the Father who is described as the one who is, was, and is to come (eternal). Additionally, it is from the seven Spirits which must refer to the Holy Spirit. "Seven" is used to denote the completeness or universality of his work.[7]

Commentators are divided about whether verse 8 refers to Christ or the Father. While the points may well apply to Christ, here they seem to refer to the Father. "The Greek term for

---

1 Joseph Henry Thayer, *A Greek-English Lexicon of the New Testament*, 62.
2 Compare Revelation 22:6, 10.
3 Ray Summers, *Worthy is the Lamb*, 99.
4 Homer Hailey, *Revelation, An Introduction and Commentary*, 96.
5 W. E. Vine, *Vine's Complete Expository Dictionary of Old and New Testament Words*, 2:575.
6 *ibid.*, 99.
7 Since the Father (v. 4) and Jesus the Son (v. 5) are mentioned, we take this to refer to the Holy Spirit. Thus, all three personalities of the Godhead send the greetings to the churches.

Almighty (*pantokrator*) appears eight other times in Revelation and applies to the Father (4:8; 11:17; 15:3; 16:7, 14; 19:15; 21:22; translated 'omnipotent' in 19:6). A consistent application demands that it be ascribed here to the Father."[8] Here he is called the Alpha (first letter of the Greek alphabet) and the Omega (the last of the Greek alphabet). This affirms God's eternal nature. Being the Almighty (cf. 4:11), he is in control and over all.

From Christ (vv. 5-8). Seven descriptions are given of the Christ.

1. Faithful witness (v. 5). The testimony he bears from the Father (cf. v. 1) is true and reliable.

2. Firstborn from the dead (v. 5). This refers to his resurrection. He is not the first to be raised from the dead, but the first to be raised never to die again.

3. Ruler over the kings of the earth (v. 5). He has power and dominion over all the kings and rulers (including Domitian who seems, at the moment, to have the upper hand). This tells us that God is in control and will be victorious (cf. 17:14). This point alone should bring comfort to the distressed.

4. Loved us and washed us from sin (v. 5). If Jesus loved us enough to die for us and cleanse us with his blood, surely he will see his people through their trials.

5. Made us kings and priests (v. 6). We have been made a kingdom of priest (cf. Exo. 19:6). We have been made as royalty! Would the one who made us kings and priests abandon his people in the midst of tribulation?

6. To him be glory and dominion forever and ever (v. 6). Here we see the lasting dominion and glory of Christ in contrast to the temporary lordship of any one of the Roman emperors.

7. Is coming in the clouds (v. 7). Jesus the Christ is coming again in the clouds (Acts 1:9).

John's Vision of Christ (vv. 9-20)

Where John was – Patmos (v. 9). John identifies himself as a companion in tribulation. He was suffering just as they were. He had been banished to the island of Patmos. This was a "small island in the Aegean Sea, located about 35 miles west of the city of Miletus off the coast of Asia Minor. Patmos is about 10 miles long and 6 miles wide at its northern end, and consists of rocky volcanic hills."[9] John said he was there "for the word of God"[10] (because of his allegiance to God's word).

Vision of Christ (vv. 10-18). This section reveals two things: how and when John had a vision (v. 10), and what he heard and saw (vv. 11-18).

1. How and when John had a vision (v. 10). John said he was "in the Spirit", meaning he was under the power and influence of the Spirit and thus taken into a vision. Ezekiel had a

---

8 Robert Harkrider, *Revelation*, Truth Commentaries 8.
9 W. A. Elwell, and B. J. Beitzel, *Baker Encyclopedia of the Bible*, 1620.
10 Compare Revelation 6:9; 20:4.

similar experience (Ezek. 3:12, 14; 8:3; 11:24; 37:1; 43:5). This vision took place on the "Lord's day,"[11] a day of worship—the first day of the week.[12]

2. What John heard and saw (vv. 11-18). John heard a voice as a loud trumpet (v. 11), suggesting a clear signal and call for attention. The voice said, "I am the Alpha and the Omega, the First and the Last" (v.11). His eternal nature is the same as the Father's (cf. v. 8). This affirms that he indeed is in control of all.

When John turned to see from where the voice was coming, he saw seven golden lampstands. He then saw one like the Son of Man (v. 13).[13] Here Christ is pictured as being in the midst of the churches as their controller and ruler.

The garment he wore (v. 13) presented him as a priest. Wayne Jackson observes that this is "a clear suggestion of the priesthood of Christ."[14] His hair was white like wool and snow (v. 14). This may imply holiness, purity as well as wisdom. His eyes were like flames of fire (v. 15). His vision was penetrating. Because he is the Alpha and Omega, he is omniscient. His feet were like fine brass (v. 15). This may allude to strength wherein he is able to tread over his enemies. His voice was like the sound of many waters (v. 15). Perhaps this symbolizes his authority and power that commands attention.

In his right hand he had seven stars as if they were jewels strung together (v. 16). He has them in his control. Their destiny is in his hand. From his mouth there was a two-edged sword (v. 16), telling of the power of his work (cf. Heb. 4:12) and that he was ready to make war and judge his enemies. His countenance was shining (v. 16).

There can be no doubt that John's mind had to, at some point, reflect back upon the scene of the transfiguration (Matt. 17:1-13).

John's reaction was that he fell down as dead (v. 17a). He was overwhelmed. However, he was comforted by the Lord when he laid his hand on him and said, "Do not be afraid; I am the first and the last" (v. 17b). Only the enemies of the Lord have reason to fear. Furthermore, he said that he was the one who was dead and is alive again thus having the keys of Hades and death (v. 18). So, if in this persecution by Rome some should lose their lives (and they did), there is no reason to fear, for Christ has the keys of Hades and death!

Commission to write (vv. 11, 19). At the beginning and the end of the vision John was commissioned to write what he saw. What he would write pertained to the things that "are" and the "things which will take place after this" (v. 19). That is, concerning the present distress and the future victory.

Explanation of the vision (v. 20). The Lord now explains what John just saw. The seven stars are the seven angels of the seven churches. But to what does "angels" refer? Some think it means the elders. Some think it is a messenger. Hailey thinks it refers to the inward life or

---

11 Not to be confused with the "day of the Lord" (a day of reckoning).
12 The first day of the week is the day the Lord was raised from the dead (Matt. 28:1ff), the day the church began (Acts 2), the day the disciples worshipped (Acts 20:7; 1 Cor. 16:1-2).
13 A reference to Jesus Christ (Matt. 8:2; 9:6) that emphasizes his humanity.
14 Wayne Jackson, *Revelation*, 30.

spirit of the congregation.[15] The idea of a messenger[16] seems to make sense.[17] The seven letters (chapters 2-3) were each addressed to the "angel of the church in..." but then the churches were urged to hear. The messenger may be elders, influential leaders, or someone who is responsible for how things were going within the churches. The seven lampstands are the seven churches.

The point of the vision is that Christ holds the future and destiny of the churches in his hand. Ray Summers gave this summary, "A living, holy, majestic, omniscient, authoritative, powerful Christ stands in the midst of the churches, holds their destiny in his hand and says: 'Stop fearing, I was dead. I am alive forever. More than that, I hold in my hand the keys of death and the grave. You should not fear to go any place to which I hold the key.'"[18]

Questions

1. When would the events discussed in the book of Revelation take place? _____
   _____

2. What does "signified" mean? _____
   _____

3. What point of encouragement would be learned from the greeting of grace (v. 4)? __
   _____
   _____

4. Why would the Holy Spirit be referred to as the seven spirits? _____
   _____
   _____

5. Does verse 8 refer to Christ or the Father? What evidence would you give? _____
   _____
   _____

6. How would God's people being made kings and priests encourage them in the midst of persecution? _____
   _____
   _____

7. Why was John on the island of Patmos? _____
   _____

8. What does it mean that John was "in the Spirit" (v. 10)? _____
   _____
   _____

---

15 *ibid.*, 116.
16 Footnote of the NKJV says "messenger." Also, Youngs Literal Translation (YLT) uses "messengers" instead of angels in Revelation 1:20.
17 The word for angel (angelos) means messenger (W. E. Vines).
18 *ibid.*, 105.

9. Describe the vision that John saw (vv. 10-18)? _____
_____
_____

10. What is the point of John's vision of Christ? _____
_____
_____

Revelation 2:1-7
Lesson 3
Letter to the Church at Ephesus
The Church that Left its First Love

Outline

I. **Identification of the Author** (v. 1)

II. **Commendation** (vv. 2-3, 6)

III. **Condemnation** (v. 4)

IV. **Plea to Repent** (v. 5)

V. **Promise if Overcome** (v. 7)

Key Verse that Summarizes the Chapter

Revelation 2:4

Nevertheless I have this against you, that you have left your first love.

We will look at each of the seven letters in a separate lesson. Though the letters are short, they are full of lessons that help the people of God today. Some of these churches were good (no condemnation given). Smyrna and Philadelphia fit that bill. Four of the seven were good and bad (received both commendation and condemnation). Those churches were found at Ephesus, Pergomas, Thyatira, and Sardis. One church was bad (received only condemnation – no praise). That church was at Laodicea.

Most of us would like to be in a good church (no condemnation at all). None of us would want to be in a church that was bad (no commendation). In reality, most of us are in a congregation that is both good and bad. The problems these churches faced are not much different from the problems we have today. We see problems of worldliness, false doctrine, indifference, materialism and compromise. No doubt, a study of these seven letters is practical.

Each of the letters follows a similar format (as seen in the outline above). Each begins with (1) identification of the author followed by (2) commendation (if there is any). Then there is (3) condemnation (if it is needed) and (4) a plea to repent (if there is condemnation). Each ends with (5) a promise if they overcome (endure).

The church at Ephesus received a letter that said "you have left your first love." In essence it said, "Your fire is gone!"

Identification of the Author (v. 1)

What is said in this letter is from the one who holds the seven stars in his right hand and walks in the midst of the seven golden lampstands (v.1). What is said (good or bad) is stated by the one who holds the destiny of the church in his hand. The Lord sees all and knows all. He has full knowledge of the interworkings of this church.

Its History

"Ephesus was the third largest city in the Roman empire. Its population is estimated to have been around 250,000 during the time of early Christianity."[1] Our appreciation for the condition of this church at the time of this letter will be enhanced if we are reminded of its rich history. Today, when we learn of a congregation's past (the preachers who have worked with them, the reputation of the elders, influential members that are there), we feel we know a lot about that church.

The following is a list of things that happened in the city or concerned the church at Ephesus.

1. Paul visited Ephesus briefly on his second missionary journey (Acts 18:18-21). He went to the synagogue and taught, but quickly moved on leaving Aquila and Priscilla there.

2. Aquila and Priscilla corrected Apollos (Acts 18:24-28). Apollos came and taught at Ephesus but only knew the baptism of John. Aquila and Priscilla corrected his understanding.

3. Twelve (who had previously been baptized) were converted (Acts 19:1-7). On Paul's third journey he came back to Ephesus and found twelve (who only knew John's baptism) and taught them to be baptized in the name of the Lord.

4. Many were converted on Paul's third missionary trip (Acts 19:8-20). Their conversion took place in the midst of controversy (vv. 8-16). Paul had to move his teaching to another location due to the opposition (v. 9). When exorcist failed in their attempt to cast out spirits and were exposed, many were lead to obey the gospel (vv. 11-20). Those who responded to the gospel burned their books showing their repentance (vv. 18-19).[2] Paul stayed with this church for three years (Acts 20:31).

5. The idol craftsmen caused a riot because of the preaching of Paul (Acts 19:2-41). Demetrius, a silversmith, stirred the crowd into a tizzy because the preaching of Paul was a threat to his business of making shrines.

6. Paul met with the Ephesian elders at Melitus (Acts 20:38). Paul reviewed his past work and warned them of the dangers in the future. The weeping and respect shown toward these elders when he left (vv. 37-38), tells us of the caliber of men who served as elders.

7. Paul may have visited again after being released from prison (1 Tim. 1:3).

---

1   Seal, D. (2012, 2013, 2014, 2015). Ephesus. In J. D. Barry, D. Bomar, D. R. Brown, R. Klippenstein, D. Mangum, C. Sinclair Wolcott, ... W. Widder (Eds.), *The Lexham Bible Dictionary*. Bellingham, WA: Lexham Press.
2   Consider their enthusiasm and zeal for the Lord in contrast to their present condition (Rev. 2:4).

8. Paul wrote a letter to the Ephesian church (Ephesians).

9. Timothy worked with the church at Ephesus (1 Tim. 1:3).

Indeed, this is a church with a very rich history.

Its Strong Qualities

The church at Ephesus had many admirable qualities.

Works (v. 2). This is what they do in the service of the Lord. "Works may be either good or bad, here they appear to be good."[3] This was an active church. They didn't just study about what they should do, they took action. They didn't just talk about their responsibilities, they worked. They did more than plan, they followed through with their plans.

Labor (v. 2). Labor (toil, ESV, ASV) is strenuous wearing labor. "'Toil' lies deeper than works. The word translated toil has reference to the effort that produces work at the cost of pain. They were working at the price of great difficulty."[4] This, indeed, was an aggressive church.

Patience (vv. 2, 3). The Lord took note of their "patient endurance" (v. 2, ESV). They had persevered (v. 3), persisting in the toil and stayed when the burden got heavy. "In patience they did not give up when things went bad or when someone criticized, mocked or ridiculed them."[5] This was a determined church.

Doctrinally correct (vv. 2, 6). They could not bear evil men (v. 2). "The evil men were detected, convicted and expelled."[6] They had exposed false apostles (v. 2). They hated the deeds of the Nicolaitans (v. 6).[7] This was a sound church.

Thus far, we are impressed with this church. They are an active church, an aggressive church, a determined church, and a doctrinally sound church. What could be wrong with such a church?

"This entire commendation leaves one inclined to question if there could be anything wrong in such a church. It carried on its services in the face of difficulties; it rejected false teachers; it hated sin; it did not grow weary in the Lord's work."[8]

Its Problem

In spite of all the strong qualities, there was indeed a problem – they left their first love (v. 4).

The place of love. Let's consider the importance of the thing they lost.

Love is essential. We must love God (Matt. 22:37). There must be a love of the truth (2 Thess. 2:10-12). Love for one another is required (Rom. 13:8).

---

3   Homer Hailey, *Revelation, An Introduction and Commentary*, 121.
4   Ray Summers, *Worthy is the Lamb*, 109.
5   Robert Harkrider, *Revelation*, 26.
6   Foy E. Wallace, Jr., *The Book of Revelation*, 86.
7   Little is known about who the Nicolaitans were. They taught false doctrine (v. 15).
8   Ray Summers, *ibid.*, 110.

Love produces action. The context shows that if they change they will start *doing* their first works (vv. 4-5). Love causes us to keep God's commands (1 John 5:3).

Without love we are nothing (1 Cor. 13).

Love and hate must be balanced. While the Ephesians had a proper hatred for error (v. 6), they did not seem to balance it with a love for what was right (v. 4).

Their first love was left behind (v. 4). They left their first love. "The honeymoon is over."[9] They were "loyal but lacking."[10] "In form, this was still a 'sound church' which fended off false doctrine, but the fire had gone out. There is much more to serving God than adherence to mechanical traditional routine."[11] Their fire was gone. Their love, enthusiasm, and excitement had vanished! What a far cry from the zeal shown when they burned their books!

This is a common problem. It is not uncommon to find those who are not excited about being Christians, nor enthused about worshipping God. It is not unusual for there to be a lack of fervency in our actions or zeal for learning and growing.

It is possible to be stronger in our opposition to sin and error than we are in our love for truth and right. It is not enough to abhor evil, we must cleave to that which is good (Rom. 12:9). "They had set out to be defenders of the faith, arming themselves with the heroic virtues of truth and courage, only to discover that in the battle they had lost the one quality without which all others are worthless...[Z]eal for Christian truth may obliterate the one truth that matters, that God is love. John is a rigorist who shares the hatred of heresy which he attributes both to the church of Ephesus and to the church's Lord; but he recognized the appalling danger of a religion prompted more by hate than by *love.*"[12]

Pulpit Commentary observed, "But it is possible to hate what Christ hates without loving what he loves. It is possible to hate false doctrine and lawlessness, and yet be formal and dead one's self."[13]

We are often stronger in our stand against worldliness than we are in our effort to develop godliness. We could be stronger in opposing sin than we are in saving sinners. It may be that our opposition to instrumental music outweighs our stand for singing. Many oppose bringing an instrument in, but never open their mouths to sing. We are sometimes more eager to expose a brother than we are in restoring the erring. Some are stronger in their stance against divorce than they are in being for marriage. It is not uncommon for a couple to stand opposed to getting a divorce, but do little or nothing to have a marriage patterned after God's word. Some are stronger in their opposition to women's liberation than they are in being keepers at home. We can easily focus more on how forsaking the assembly is a sin than we do on worshipping God.

---

9 Harkrider, *ibid.*, 25.
10 Summers, *ibid.*, 108.
11 Harkrider, *ibid.*, 28.
12 C. B. Caird, *A Commentary on the Revelation of St. John the Divine*, 31.
13 H. D. M. Spence-Jones, (Ed.), *Revelation*, 58. London; New York: Funk & Wagnalls Company.

Its Future

They were about to lose their identity. If they didn't change, and soon, their candlestick was about to be removed (v. 5). Soon, they no longer would be the "Lord's church." It is decision time! They can't stay in this lull or rut any longer.

It is not uncommon to find a church that has problems. Some are major and some are minor. Sometimes those problems are simply that the church is in a lull, a rut or the fire has gone out. When such is the case, it is time for change. It is time to act. It is time to do something.

The problems are curable. Often, when a church has some problems people are ready to leave, thinking things will never get better.

1. It could be fixed. "Surely in this milder denunciation we may see a proof that the evil in Ephesus was curable...But the cooling of the first Ephesian enthusiasm was a failing that lies in human nature. The failing can be corrected, the enthusiasm may be revived."[14]

2. They must repent. Repentance is prompted by memory (v. 5). "The lever of repentance is memory (Ps. 137:5-6; Luke 15:17-21)."[15] Once they remember, repentance (change of mind) should follow (v. 5). The result is a change of life ("and do the first works", v. 5a). Thus, they were told to remember, repent and return.

Questions

1. How large was the city of Ephesus? _____

2. Who were some of the notable people who had been at Ephesus? _____

3. How did the church at Ephesus start? _____

4. What value is there in looking at the history of the church and its beginning? _____

5. What strong qualities do you see in the church at Ephesus? _____

6. What was the problem with this church? _____

---

14 W.M. Ramsay, *The Letters to the Seven Churches of Asia*, 244.
15 Harkrider, *ibid.*, 28.

7. What does "left your first love" mean? _____
   _____

8. How is love and hate to be balanced? _____
   _____
   _____

9. List some present day examples of leaving our first love. _____
   _____
   _____
   _____

10. How does memory relate to repentance? _____
    _____
    _____

Revelation 2:8-11

Lesson 4
Letter to the Church at Symrna
The Church Under Presssure

Outline

I. **Identification of the Author (v. 8)**

II. **Commendation (v. 9)**

III. **Promise if Overcome (vv. 10-11)**

Key Verse that Summarizes the Chapter

Revelation 2:10

Do not fear any of those things which you are about to suffer. Indeed, the devil is about to throw *some* of you into prison, that you may be tested, and you will have tribulation ten days. Be faithful until death, and I will give you the crown of life.

The church at Smyrna received a letter saying the circumstances are bad and are going to get worse. Not exactly what any church wants to hear. This church was under pressure. Yet, it was one of the two good churches (the other being Philadelphia) that received no condemnation. This is the shortest of the seven letters (only four verses). Smyrna was a poor church (by the world's standards), but rich in faith and strength.

How the church began, we are not told. Perhaps it started when the gospel went throughout all Asia while Paul was at Ephesus (Acts 19:10).

Located just 40 miles north of Ephesus, the city of Smyrna was the birthplace for the Greek poet, Homer. "It had passed into obscurity at one time but was rebuilt by Alexander the Great and Antigonus."[1] The city was known for idolatry. A shrine was erected to Roma, a Roman goddess, around 195 B.C..[2] Smyrna was chosen, over several competing cities, for the site of a temple to Tiberius (Roman emperor, 14-37 A.D.). Thus, it became a center for emperor worship, which was compulsory under Domitian.

Their Challenges

Tribulation (v. 9). This is a reference to the persecution they are already experiencing. The word for tribulation literally means "pressure." "The word used here for tribulation is a

---

1 Ray Summers, *Worthy is the Lamb*, 112.
2 Homer Hailey, *Revelation, An Introduction and Commentary*, 125.

word which pictures the grinding of the wheat at the mill or the crushing of grapes in the wine press. It is outside pressure which appears at first sight to crush or ruin, but it proved to make the grain (as flour) and the grapes (as wine) to be of greater service."[3] Thus, the pressure is on!

Poverty (v. 9). This seems to be associated with the persecution. "The tribulation was probably persecution, which helped to intensify the poverty of the Christians (James 2:5; 1 Cor. 1:26; 2 Cor. 6:10; 8:2)."[4] It may include economic pressure from some influential Jews who were compromisers.[5] Summers concludes it involves confiscation of property by Domitian as a means of persecution.[6]

Blasphemy (v. 9). Their name and character was being slandered. Perhaps this refers to those Jews who had escaped persecution through compromise. When those who should stand with you compromise, it adds pressure.

Caesar worship was more political than religious, as least from Rome's point of view. One could burn incense to Caesar saying, "Caesar is Lord" and then worship who or how he may, just as long as he was still loyal to Rome. Apparently, some Jews, who claimed to believe in the one true God, had compromised by submitting to the request of Rome. That was blasphemy. Since true Christians would not do the same, they would be labeled as traitors by these compromisers.

Anytime people, who should stand, compromise, it adds pressure to the one who tries to stand strong. When you tell others that you don't dance, drink, dress immodest or go to some of the movies, the people of the world could easily cite some "Christian" they know (who even worships with you) that doesn't seem to have a problem with doing those things. The same goes for missing services, for working overtime or playing sports. When you explain to the boss or coach that you can't do that, they may retort that others who claim to believe as you do have no problem missing services. It adds to the pressure.

Their Strength

Works (v. 9). Since there was no condemnation given to this church, these works must have been good works. They were active. Their faith was not dead. They didn't merely talk the talk of doing good, they walked the walk!

Rich (v. 9). They were rich in what really mattered. They were rich in faith, character and works.

Their Encouragement

The resurrection of Christ gives hope (v. 8). Jesus is described as the one "who was dead, and came to life" (v. 8). "The Lord's victory over death and His present position should inspire confidence within a church that was about to suffer imprisonment and tribulation even unto death...For He who became dead is now alive and able to give victory over every obstacle, even death."[7]

---

3   Summers, *ibid.*, 103.
4   A. T. Robertson, *Word Pictures in the New Testament* (Rev. 2:9). Nashville, TN: Broadman Press.
5   See the next section on blasphemy.
6   *ibid.*, 104.
7   Homer Hailey, *ibid.*, 125, 127.

God knows all (v. 8). If Jesus is the First and the Last, then he is all knowing. He knows the truth about his servants. He knows what they really are at heart. He knows the truth about the enemies of God and the servants of God. God is paying attention to what is going on in this struggle.

Can overcome (v. 11). The letter ends with the promise that the one who overcomes will not be hurt in the second death. Thus, it is possible to endure the trials they are facing and were about to face. "The beauty of this city, which rivaled Ephesus, was the beauty of a resurrection. Seven hundred years before, old Smyrna had been destroyed, and had lain in ruins for three centuries. The city of John's time was one which had risen from the dead. And resurrection was to be the experience of its church also."[8]

Their Test (v. 10)

Verse 10 tells this church that their bad circumstance is about to get worse. They are about to face a greater test of their faith.

The source. The trials coming their way are coming from the devil himself. God allows us to be tempted and tried, but is not the cause behind them.

The treatment. Three words are found in this verse that describe how they will be treated. They will suffer, be cast into prison[9], and face tribulation[10].

The duration. Is this going to last forever? No, the text says ten days. Not literally nine plus one. The meaning is that it will be complete and full, but will come to an end. There is hope that they can overcome (v. 11).

The reaction. How should the saints in this church react to the severe trials they face? They were told to "be faithful" anyway – even under this pressure. The persecution and suffering would be no excuse for a lack of faithfulness.

Note carefully that their faithfulness was to be "unto death" (v. 10). Not just *until* death, but even *to the point* of death.

Polycarp (70 -155 AD) was a direct pupil of the apostle John. He was martyred on Sunday, February 23, 155. Being from Smyrna, he likely would have been present when this letter was read to the church. He was charged to worship Caesar and renounce Christ. His response was, "Fourscore and six years have I served him, and he has never done me injury; how then can I now blaspheme my King and savior?"[11] Consequently, he was threatened with fire. His response was, "You threaten me with fire which burns for an hour, and is then extinguished, but you know nothing of the fire of the coming judgment and eternal punishment, reserved for the ungodly. Why are you waiting? Bring on whatever you want."[12] Polycarp was then burned alive at the stake. That is what it means to be "faithful unto death" (v. 10)!

---

8 Michael Wilcock, *The Message of Revelation*, 45.
9 This probably doesn't refer to literally being thrown into a prison. Perhaps it refers to a trial, arrest, being fined, exiled or even death.
10 Here again the word means a crushing pressure from outside as seen previously.
11 https://www.christianhistoryinstitute.org/incontext/article/polycarp-testimony/.
12 https://www.christianhistoryinstitute.org/study/module/polycarp/.

Think about how Polycarp's example compares with our half-hearted service, missing a lot of worship, our casual and carefree spirit, the fact that we don't have time to do what we should, or our lack of spirituality.

The result. If these saints are faithful until death, they will receive a crown of life (crowned with victory in heaven, v. 10). If they endure the tribulation, they will not be hurt in the second death (v. 11). The first death is one's physical death. The second death refers to eternal damnation (cf. Rom. 6:23).

Questions

1. How did the church at Smyrna begin? _____
   _____

2. In one line, what did the letter to Smyrna say? _____
   _____

3. What challenges did this church face? _____
   _____
   _____

4. What does the word "tribulation" tell us about what this church faced? _____
   _____

5. How does someone else's compromise put pressure on the faithful? _____
   _____
   _____

6. In what way were those at Smyrna rich? _____
   _____

7. How did the resurrection of Christ encourage them? _____
   _____
   _____

8. What does "faithful unto death" (v. 10) mean? _____
   _____

9. What does the "ten days" suggest about their suffering? _____
   _____

10. For class discussion: in what ways does Polycarp's faithfulness contrast to our lack of diligence today? _____
    _____
    _____

Revelation 2:12-17
Lesson 5
Letter to the Church at Pergamos
The Church That Compromised

Outline

I. Identification of the Author (v. 12)

II. Commendation (v. 13)

III. Condemnation (vv. 14-15)

IV. Plea to Repent (v. 16)

V. Promise if Overcome (v. 17)

Key Verse that Summarizes the Chapter

Revelation 2:14

But I have a few things against you, because you have there those who hold the doctrine of Balaam, who taught Balak to put a stumbling block before the children of Israel, to eat things sacrificed to idols, and to commit sexual immorality.

The church at Pergamos received a letter saying you live where Satan dwells and you have struck a compromise. This was one of the churches that was both good and bad (receiving both commendation and condemnation).

Pergamos[1] was located about 30 miles north of Smyrna. It was the northernmost of the seven cites mentioned in Revelation 2-3. With the help of Rome, the residents of Pergamos expelled Antiochus, III (King of Syria) in 190 B.C. In 133 B.C., the King of Pergamos (Attalus, III) gave the city and his entire kingdom to the Roman government upon his death. In 29 B.C. a temple was erected to Augustus (Roman emperor who was honored as being divine). This was the first temple devoted to emperor worship.[2] Of all the seven cities, Pergamos was perhaps the worst due to this environment.

---

1   "The proper form of the name is *Pergamum*" (M. R. Vincent, *Word Studies in the New Testament*, 2:446).
2   See Homer Hailey, *Revelation, An Introduction and Commentary*, 129.

Its Strength

This church has several impressive and commendable things to notice.

Works (v. 13). These "works" must be good since the condemnation doesn't come until later (v. 14). This is an active church. They were busy. This is a group that did more than think, talk and plan. They followed through with their plans.

Hold fast to my name (v. 13). They well understood that Jesus is Lord of lords (cf. Rev. 17:14) and acknowledged no other lord (i.e. Caesar). This would include recognizing his authority (Acts 4:7). This church held fast, stuck to it and did not waver.

Did not deny my faith (v. 13). They did not deny the faith that Jesus taught his disciples to believe (the objective faith, Phil. 1:27; Jude 3). Neither did they deny the faith that Jesus taught his followers to have (the subjective faith, Heb. 10:39–11:1). They never once backed down.

Faithful in spite of martyrdom (v. 13). We know very little about Antipas. He must have been a member of the church at Pergamos in that he was "killed among you" (v. 13). While the name Antipas most likely refers to a specific person, it is possible (as some argue) that it stood for all who had died as martyrs. "That he was the bishop of the church and was burned alive in a heated metal image of a bull during the days of Domitian is a legend that appeared in the tenth century."[3] Even that did not shake them.

Its Temptation

The fact that Pergamos is where "Satan's throne is" and "where Satan dwells" (v. 13) means that the people of God who lived there faced temptation. They were surrounded by pagans, heathens and worldliness. Satan's "throne" suggests that his influence controlled the people of the city. How hard it must have been to live in such a city. There obviously would have been a temptation to compromise. "Everyone has a choice to make. Either compromise faith and blend with the evil, or face the ridicule from the majority as foolish, fanatical, and too radical about faith."[4]

The temptation they faced could be overcome and conquered (v. 17). "The principle of the Christian life is not escape, but conquest. It may be that we often feel it would be very much easier to be a Christian in some other place and in some other circumstances, amongst people who are more sympathetic...If in the early days Christians had run away every time they were confronted with an engagement very difficult, there would have been no chance of a world for Christ."[5]

Its Weakness

Those that hold the doctrine of Balaam (v. 14). We read of Balaam in Numbers 25:1-8 where he seduced Israel with harlots to cause them to sin so that they would not be blessed. A little later the text said, "Look, these women caused the children of Israel, through the counsel of Balaam, to trespass against the Lord in the incident of Peor, and there was a plague among

---

3   R. C. H. Lenski, *The Interpretation of St. John's Revelation*, 105.
4   Robert Harkrider, *Revelation*, 36.
5   William Barclay, *The Revelation of John*, 1:112-113.

the congregation of the LORD" (Num. 31:16). Balaam loved "wages of unrighteousness" (2 Pet. 2:15). Jude warned of those who "run greedily in the error of Balaam for profit" (Jude 11). The doctrine of Balaam was simply a doctrine of compromise.

Those that hold the doctrine of the Nicolaitans (v. 15). We do not know who the Nicolaitans were (cf. 2:6). Some have thought this is a reference to the Gnostics who taught that what the flesh does is immaterial, thus they could compromise (burning incense to Caesar) to secure their own safety. However, we cannot be sure who they were. Barclay observed, "The fault of the Nicolaitans was that they were seeking to adjust Christianity to the level of the world rather than lift the world to the level of Christianity. In other words, they were following a policy of compromise simply and solely to save themselves from trouble they were afraid and unwilling to face."[6]

In reality, the doctrine of Balaam and the doctrine of the Nicolaitans was the same doctrine. "It is significant to mention here that the term *Nicolaitane* is the Greek equivalent of the name *Balaam* in the Hebrew, and they both meant 'the destroyer of the people.'"[7] "Since the names mean the same, Jesus probably had the same error in mind."[8]

Tolerating those who held this doctrine. Consider those who were being addressed. "It was not dictated to those preaching and practicing cultural relevance. It was sent to those who had remained true but were extending their fellowship to the participants of error."[9] This church had as much (if not more) of a problem with *toleration* of those in error as with those who were in error themselves. That is often the case today. Many errors are taught among brethren. Those who teach the error are not the only problem. Those who tolerate and fellowship them create just as much of a problem, if not more.

The Need

Repent (v. 16). They needed to change. They needed to change the way they thought and the way they lived. Those who held to the doctrine of compromise needed to cease. There was a need to cease tolerating those in error.

Do so quickly (v. 16). God's patience was running out. There was no time for delay. The need was urgent. Souls were at stake.

Its Motivation

What is presented in this letter to motivate this church to change the things that needed changing?

The authority and power of Christ (vv. 12, 16). Christ is the one with the two edged sword (v. 12). He will fight against them with the sword of his mouth (v. 16). "The power of Rome might be satanically powerful; the power of the Risen Lord was greater yet."[10] That alone should motivate them.

---

6   *ibid.*, I:115.
7   Foy E. Wallace, Jr., *The Book of Revelation*, 93.
8   Dan Winkler, *Spiritual Sword*, 29:1, October 1997, 23.
9   Winkler, *ibid.*, 23.
10 William Barclay, *The Revelation of John*, 111.

The knowledge of Christ—He knows all (v. 13). Christ is omniscient. He knows their works, and whether they held fast or denied his faith. Nothing can be hidden from Christ.

Blessing if overcome (v. 17). Those who endure and overcome were promised hidden manna to eat. Just as God provided for his people in the wilderness by giving them manna from heaven, God promised to supply their every need. The manna was "hidden." "Kept either within or before the ark of the covenant (cf. Exod. 16:33; 1 Kings 8:9; Heb. 9:4), it was hidden from view." [11]

Additionally, the ones who overcome would be given a white stone as a sign of victory or acquittal. "Pergamum engaged in the mining of white stone and the use of it as a commercial product. The use of a piece of this stone with a name on it was varied."[12] Four such uses are suggested by Summers:

1. A white stone would be given to a man justly acquitted to prove he was free of the charges made against him.

2. A white stone would be given to a slave to prove his freedom and his citizenship.

3. A white stone would be given to the winner of a race to prove he overcame opposition.

4. A white stone would be given to a warrior returning home from battle to honor his victory.

Ample reasons were given for this church to make the changes that were needed.

Questions

1. What commendation was given to this church? _____
_____

2. What condemnation was given to this church? _____
_____

3. Why was Pergamos considered the place where Satan dwells? _____
_____
_____

4. What do we learn from this letter about dealing with church problems versus running from them? _____
_____
_____

---

11   Homer Hailey, *ibid.*,133.
12   Summers, *ibid.*, 116.

5. Who was Anitpas and what do we know about him? _____
_____
_____

6. In what way did some in this church try to compromise? _____
_____
_____

7. What is said or implied in this letter about toleration of compromisers and those in error? _____
_____

8. What is the hidden manna? _____
_____

9. What is the white stone? _____
_____

10. What was this church told to do about the problem of compromise? _____
_____
_____

Revelation 2:18-29
Lesson 6
Letter to the Church at Thyatira
The Church That Was Tolerant

Outline

I. Identification of the Author (v. 18)

II. Commendation (v. 19)

III. Condemnation (vv. 20-21)

IV. Plea to Repent (vv. 22-23)

V. Promise if Overcome (vv. 24-29)

Key Verse that Summarizes the Chapter

Revelation 2:20

Nevertheless I have a few things against you, because you allow that woman Jezebel, who calls herself a prophetess, to teach and seduce My servants to commit sexual immorality and eat things sacrificed to idols.

The church at Thyatira received a letter saying you have allowed the wicked to do their work. This made it a tolerant church. This congregation, like Ephesus and Pergamos, was both good and bad (receiving both commendation and condemnation).

Thyatira was located in the Lycus River Valley. Little is said elsewhere in the text about the city. Lydia was from Thyatira (Acts 16:14).

The Messenger (vv. 18, 23)

Jesus, the messenger of all these letters, is here described in terms not found in the other six letters.

Son of God (v. 18). He is deity – God (John 5:17-18). He is the judge of all in that God has committed all judgment to the Son (John 5:22). The one who sent a message saying they needed to repent is the judge of all the earth.

Eyes like a flame of fire (v. 18). This may refer to his anger when he saw the problems in this and the other churches. It could refer to the penetrating nature of his vision.

Feet like fine brass (v. 18). This might suggest the firmness of his stand against sin and error – the very kind of stand that needed to be taken at Thyatira. Perhaps the beauty of his stand is indicated (i.e. that it is better to take a firm stand than compromise).

Searches the mind and heart (v. 23). As Christ deals with the problems at Thyatira, all churches would learn that he searches the minds and hearts. He knows all. He examines the heart fully before judgment.

What a sobering thought that someday we will stand before the judge of all the earth who is God himself, whose anger is stirred by sin and error, whose stand against ungodliness is firm and who knows our most secret thoughts. A reminder of that should move us, as it should have the church at Thyatira, to get things in order.

The Strength (v. 19)

This church had many commendable things about it. In fact, a slightly longer list is presented here than in those we have already seen.

Works. This apparently was an active church that was busy. There was as much doing as planning, talking or discussing what needed to be done. We hope this is true of all churches today.

Love. This must include a love for God, His word and His people. With that love, other responsibilities fall into place (Rom. 13:10).

Service. Their love drove them to serve God (Acts 27:25) and serve others (Gal. 5:13). Their service certainly made them an active group.

Faith. Faith comes by hearing the word of God (Rom. 10:17). They believed, based upon the evidence they had seen. This tells of their reaction to the word. Not all who claim to be Christians believe the revealed will of God (cf. Acts 27:25). True faith leads to obedience (Rom. 1:5; 16:26).

Patience. Because their faith was real, they could endure and persevere. Their faithfulness and steadfastness was attested to in this commendation.

Last is greater than first. Concerning their works, the last was greater than the first. They had grown and progressed. They were doing more now than they had at first. Often, the opposite is true. Many churches look back and remember a time when the members were more active than at the present.

This was an impressive group. This is just what one wants in a local church today. They were active, loving, and serving. They had faith, patience and were growing. However, the next verse identified a problem.

The Weakness (v. 20)

The church at Thyatira was *tolerant* in that they allowed a woman named Jezebel to seduce some of the people of God to commit sexual immorality and eat things sacrificed to idols.

Who is Jezebel? Jezebel was the wicked wife of the evil king Ahab who stirred him up (1 Kings 21:25). Here the name is used symbolically like "Balaam" was (Rev. 2:14). It may refer to a group that was a faction within the church. Or, it may refer to some woman who had an evil influence like unto Jezebel. Whatever the case, Jezebel claimed to be a prophetess (claimed to be speaking by God or at least that her advice was in harmony with God), but was not.

Jezebel was allowed. The church at Thyatira did not teach others to commit immorality, but they tolerated one who did. There is no indication that they approved of her teaching and work. But, they tolerated it. The word "allow"[1] suggests that she could and should have been stopped. The Lord condemned the church for not taking action.

What was allowed. Jezebel taught some of the Christians to commit fornication and eat things sacrificed to idols. This could be actual literal fornication in connection with idolatry.[2] However, it could have reference to spiritual adultery. This city had its share of the trade guilds wherein its members were encouraged to participate in their social festivals that had many pagan elements.[3] One might be encouraged to participate in meals that honor idols to promote their business or trade. If one refused, their job might be in jeopardy. This Jezebel may have encouraged some to compromise their faith.

There is no evidence that either Jezebel or those she taught had quit going to services or stopped in their attempt to serve God. "The woman (or faction) referred to as Jezebel had not quit the church at Thyatira, and was not encouraging others to quit the church...Many there are who would not think of quitting the church altogether, but who compromise with the devil on first one thing and then another."[4] The problem is that the church had allowed all this to happen!

The church bore some responsibility. The church was addressed in this letter and not Jezebel. God held the church responsible for its members. The blame was not just on Jezebel, but on the church as well!

The Warning (vv. 21-23)

Their weakness demanded that warning be given. If Jezebel and her followers stood in jeopardy, so did those who tolerated them.

Rejected opportunities and refused to repent (v. 21). Jezebel had been given time to repent of her sexual immorality, but she stubbornly refused (cf. ESV). The New Century Version translated this, "but she does not want to change."

Faces judgment to come (v. 23). The Lord promisesd, "And I will give to each one of you according to your works" (v. 23). That would apply to Jezebel who led others into sin. That

---

1 ESV translates this "tolerate."
2 Erroneous teaching could encourage one to commit fornication. The errors being taught on divorce and remarriage that condone and encourage unscriptural marriages teach one to commit fornication.
3 See Homer Hailey, *Revelation, An Introduction and Commentary*, 137-138.
4 Bobby Duncan, *Spiritual Sword*, 29:1, October 1997, 25.

would include those whom she had seduced to commit sexual immorality.⁵ Those who tolerated the whole mess will be judged according to their works as well.

Punishment (vv. 22-23). Three expressions describe the punishment that is due to Jezebel and her followers. (1) She will be cast into a sickbed (v. 22). "'A bed of sickness in contrast with the bed of adultery' (Beckwith)."⁶ "Not into a bed of ease, but a bed of pain. There is evidently a purpose to contrast this with her former condition. The harlot's bed and a sickbed are thus brought together, as they are often, in fact, in the dispensations of Providence and the righteous judgments of God. One cannot be indulged without leading on, sooner or later, to the horrid sufferings of the other: and how soon no one knows."⁷

(2) She will be cast into great tribulation (v. 22) or great suffering.⁸ (3) Her children (those she has influenced) will be killed with death (v. 23).

The choice was theirs (v. 22). "Unless they repent of their deeds" tells us that any punishment for sin could be avoided with a total change of the heart. They have no one to blame but themselves.

The Assurance (vv. 24-19)

All do not compromise or sin (v. 24). There were those in the church at Thyatira who did not hold to the doctrine or practice of Jezebel. Neither had they compromised or been as tolerant as others had. How assuring to look around in a church that has some troublesome people, as well as those who tolerate them, and find that there are a few who stand strong against both.

These had not known the "depths of Satan" (v. 24). The NCV renders this, "and have not learned what some call Satan's deep secrets." There are two questions about this phrase. One, who is calling this the depths of Satan? Is it the faithful Christians or the heretics? Second, what are they actually saying? This writer cannot be sure on either question. However, Lenski's explanation makes some sense:

> It is asked whether the heretics or the Christians are the subjects and speak of "the deep things (profundities) of Satan." Some think that the expression is ironical, that, while these Gnostic heretics called them "the deep things of God," the Lord here substitutes what these things really were, namely "the deep things of Satan." It is argued on the evidence of history that no Gnostic claim is found elsewhere that purports knowing "the deep things of Satan."
>
> We take the words just as they read. The adherents of this woman spoke of "the deep things of Satan" and said that one must know them, realize what they are by experience and experiment. This justified their fornication, adultery, and eating at idol feasts. They looked down upon the innocent Christians who refused to experiment and refrained from these things. These superior heretics claimed that they killed the flesh by indulging the

---

5   Hailey makes a point that there would be those who were "her victims who have been influenced, but could yet be redeemed" (ibid., 139).
6   A. T. Robertson, *Word Pictures in the New Testament* (Rev. 2:22).
7   Albert Barnes, *Notes on the New Testament: Revelation*, 83.
8   Hailey calls this the "bed of tribulation" (ibid., 139).

flesh, claimed to plunge into filth to prove that it could not harm them, that the innocent Christians were only weak and afraid when they refused to do the same.

This sort of teaching and experiment is advocated to this day. To know the world one must plunge into the world.[9]

The Lord knows and understands (v. 24). We learn in the previous point that the Lord takes note of those who do not yield to the pressures that are upon them. The Lord assured them saying, "I will put on you no other burden." The Lord knows and understands that it is a burden for those who are striving to live right while others (who are supposed to be Christians) are not.

Can endure and overcome (vv. 25-26a). In spite of the problems Thyatira had, it was possible to "hold fast" (v. 25), overcome (v. 26), and keep the works of God (v. 26).

Rewarded (vv. 26b-29). Those who overcome will be given power over the nations (v. 26). The nations (i.e. Rome) will not control the destiny of the saints. As evidence, Psalm 2:8-9 is quoted which speaks of the power of Christ to shatter the nations that resist him. Additionally, the one who overcomes will be given "the morning star" (v. 28). This may refer to "his guidance and leadership in the dark hour of troubles and trials."[10] Or, as Hailey suggests, "He will give to the conqueror a new day; the night is almost over."[11]

Questions

1. How would the identification of the author of the letter impact the reader? _____
   _____

2. What were the points of strength in the church at Thyatira? _____
   _____

3. Who was Jezebel (that is mentioned in this letter)? _____
   _____

4. What did Jezebel do that was wrong? _____
   _____

5. What had the church at Thyatira done about Jezebel? _____
   _____

6. In what way would there be a temptation for the Christians in business in the city of Thyatira to compromise their faith? _____
   _____
   _____

---

9 R. C. H. Lenski, *The Interpretation of St. John's Revelation*, 119–120.
10 Ray Summers, *Worthy is the Lamb*, 119.
11 Hailey, *ibid.*, 142.

7. How did Jezebel react to efforts to bring her to repentance? _____
   _____

8. What three expressions describe the punishment that Jezebel was to receive? _____
   _____
   _____
   _____

9. How could other Christians not living right create a burden for the faithful? _____
   _____
   _____

10. What reward would be given to the one(s) that overcame? _____
    _____
    _____

Revelation 3:1-6
Lesson 7
Letter to the Church at Sardis
The Church That Was Dead

Outline

I. Identification of the Author (v. 1)

II. Commendation (vv. 2, 4)

III. Condemnation (vv. 1, 3)

IV. Plea to Repent (v. 3)

V. Promise if Overcome (vv. 5-6)

Key Verse that Summarizes the Chapter

Revelation 3:1

And to the angel of the church in Sardis write, These things says He who has the seven Spirits of God and the seven stars: I know your works, that you have a name that you are alive, but you are dead.

The church at Sardis may have been shocked to learn that they were dead. Surprised, perhaps, because they had many desirable qualities. This church, like Ephesus, Pergamos, and Thyatira was both good and bad (received both commendation and condemnation).

Good Qualities That Did Not Prevent Death[1]

This church died in spite of the commendable things found in their midst. The lesson to be learned for us today is that a church can have many good qualities and still be dead in the eyes of God.

Good reputation (v. 1). This church had a name that they were alive. Their works apparently had built their good name. What they had done in the past had caused others to speak well of them.

---

1 Credit given to Ed Bragwell for the four points under this section.

Churches today can have a good reputation. This might be based upon their past stand. It might be based upon some of the members that are known. It might be based upon the preacher they have or had in the past. It might be based upon how they stood on one particular issue. Some churches merely live on a name. That is, they constantly look to what they have done in the past. A church that stood strong years ago when brethren were dividing may boast of the reputation they have built. There are congregations whose names we easily recognize because of what they were ten, twenty or thirty years ago. That tells us little about their condition now.

We learn some practical things at this juncture. It is possible to have a lot of things right about a church and still be wrong. It is possible for churches to change. Sardis apparently had. Furthermore, churches are not always as they appear. It is possible to visit a church (several times) and be impressed, yet there still be problems.

Their reputation did not keep them from dying!

An active program (v 1). This church had "works" (v. 1) that were good. Thus, they were active and busy. Yet, they were dead.

It is never enough to be busy as a church. Our works must first be lawful (Matt. 7:22-23; 2 Jno. 9). Many want to attend a church that has many programs, but give little attention to whether they are scriptural or not (Col. 3:17).

Neither is it enough to be active in some things. The Lord told Sardis, "I have not found your works perfect before God," (v. 2). Their actions were not "complete" (ESV). Their "deeds were unfinished" (NIV). Indeed, the Lord takes note of the things left undone (Matt. 23:23). A church might have a good Bible class program, yet not practice church discipline. A church might be busy in a personal evangelism program, yet be soft on doctrinal or moral issues. A church may be supporting numerous preachers, but have worldliness in their midst. A church might be in a building program (more room is needed for classes or worship assemblies) while neglecting spiritual matters.

Their active program did not keep them from dying.

A peaceful atmosphere. There was no evidence of division or strife at Sardis as could be seen at Corinth (1 Cor. 1:10-11). Just because there is peace and harmony does not mean that all is well with a church. Peace must not be a toleration of sin. The church at Corinth was tolerating, for a while at least, a fornicator in their midst (1 Cor. 5). Peace must not be a toleration of error. Thyatira had allowed Jezebel to spread her error (Rev. 2:20). Error that goes unchecked leads disciples away (Acts 20:29-30; 2 Tim. 4:1-5). Peace must not be from indifference, as we will see later in the church at Laodicea (Rev. 3:16-17). Sin is no problem to those who don't care. Neither does error matter to those who are apathetic. Obviously, some love peace and harmony over truth.

Their peaceful atmosphere did not keep them from dying.

Some good members (v. 4). There were a few in Sardis living as they should (v. 4). These were the kind of really good members any church would want to have. But even that was not enough to keep this church from dying.

Good members do not answer for the sins of others. Good members do not remove the sins of others. Good members at Corinth didn't mean that there were not serious problems in that church (1 Cor. 5, 6). We learn from this letter that good members can remain pure in spite of the fact that others are not doing as they should. However, good members can change as they are influenced by those who are not good members (1 Cor. 5:6).

Having good members did not keep them from dying.

You may look around in the church where you are a member and think that this is really a good church due to the fact that there are so many good qualities that you can count. However, those may not keep that church from being dead in God's eyes.

Preventing Death and Reviving Life

What can a church do to prevent its death? What should a church do, as Sardis, that finds itself dead, to revive the life?

Be watchful (vv. 2-3). "Lit., *become awake and on the watch...Become* what thou art not."[2] They had lost their ground by carelessness. It was time to wake up.[3]

To be watchful we must take a look at where we are and where that will lead if we continue on the same path. Matthew Henry correctly said, "Whenever we are off our watch, we lose ground, and therefore must return to our watchfulness against sin, and Satan, and whatever is destructive to the life and power of godliness."[4]

We must be on guard – alert to the dangers! Constantly look back and see how we have changed.

Strengthen the things that remain (v. 2). They were to use and exercise what strength they had lest they lose it. This may refer to persons. That is, warn and strengthen them lest they become like the rest. It is more likely that it refers to deeds or works (love, faith, and service).[5] That is, strengthen what you have lest these die too! They had started, but had failed to continue as they should.

There will always be those who are doing what is right and seek to strengthen what remains. "In the lowest state of religion in a church there may be a few, perhaps quite obscure and of humble rank, who are mourning over the desolations of Zion, and who are sighing for better times."[6]

Remember and repent (v. 3). The church at Sardis was told, "Remember therefore how you have received and heard; hold fast and repent" (v. 3). They needed to remember *how* they had embraced the gospel. Perhaps, they had accepted the gospel with zeal and excitement, but that was now gone. Perhaps, the joy they once had when they heard the message was lost.

---

2 M. R. Vincent, *Word Studies in the New Testament*, 2:461.
3 The ESV has "wake up" for the word watchful.
4 *Matthew Henry's Commentary on the Whole Bible: Complete and Unabridged in One Volume*, 2468.
5 Evidence that this refers to deeds is found in the statement that immediately follows the phrase we are discussing, "for I have not found your works perfect before God."
6 Albert Barnes, *Notes on the New Testament: Revelation*, 89.

They needed to remember *what* they had heard—the truth! At least part of that message seems to have been forgotten (cf. Heb. 5:12). Likewise, part of that message was not being practiced. Once they remember how and what they heard, they must repent and go back to that.

Questions

1. What commendation was given to the church at Sardis? _____

2. What condemnation was given to the church at Sardis? _____

3. What qualities did not prevent their death? _____

4. What can be done to prevent death or revive life? _____

5. What was the reputation of this church and why would that not keep them from dying? _____

6. Why would a peaceful atmosphere not always be good for a church? _____

7. How could an active church also be dead? _____

8. What does it mean to be watchful? _____

9. What does "strengthen the things that remain" mean? _____

10. For class discussion: Could the church where you are a member be dead? What would indicate that it is possibly dead? What could be done about it if it is dead? _____

Revelation 3:7-13
Letter to the Church at Philadelphia
The Church That Was Faithful

Lesson 8

Outline

I. Identification of the Author (v. 7)

II. Commendation (vv. 8-11)

III. Promise if Overcome (vv. 12-13)

Key Verse that Summarizes the Chapter

Revelation 3:10

Because you have kept My command to persevere, I also will keep you from the hour of trial which shall come upon the whole world, to test those who dwell on the earth.

The church at Philadelphia received a letter saying, "You've done great, so keep on! You have promise and opportunity." This was a faithful church. This church and the one at Symrna were the only two that received commendation and no condemnation.

Philadelphia was located 28 miles SE of Sardis. It dates back to 159 B.C. King Attalus II Philadelphus, of Pergamum (159-138 B.C.) named it out of affection for his brother Ecumenus, II.[1] This was a "missionary" city that was suited for the purpose of spreading the Greek culture and language. It was the youngest of the seven cities.

We know nothing about the establishment or the history of the church in Philadelphia. We do know that they faced some opposition from Jews (v. 9).

The Salutation (v. 7)

The salutation identifies the qualities or characteristics of the author of the letter – Jesus Christ.

Holy. He is identified with the holiness that is true of the Father (Rev. 4:8; Psa. 111:9). This speaks of his purity. "It is not only an appellation appropriate to the Saviour, but well adapted to be employed when he is addressing the churches. Our impression of what is said to us

---

1   Philadelphia means brotherly love.

will often depend much on our idea of the character of him who addresses us, and solemnity and thoughtfulness always become us when we are addressed by a holy Redeemer."[2]

True. He is dependable. He is genuine and real. Christ is the true bread (John 6:32), the true light (John 1:9), and the true vine (John 15:1). He is true in contrast to the Jews who were not true (v. 9). He is true (he is what he claims to be) in contrast to the Roman emperor who was not who he claimed to be.

Has the key of David. He is the one in whom the promise to David's seed is fulfilled (Isa. 9:6-7; Luke 1:32-33). Eliakim was given the key of the house of David with the authority to open and shut (Isa. 22:20-22). "These powers were entrusted to him, who was an anti-type of Christ, but to Christ they belong by right."[3] Christ is the one who sits on the throne of David.

The "key" implies the power to open and shut (cf. Isa. 22) which points to the authority he exercises over his kingdom.

Summers ties these three points under the salutation together by saying, "His character of holiness and truth is his right to kingship."[4]

The Praise (vv. 8, 10)

This church only received *commendation*; no *condemnation*. They were indeed a faithful church. They had good works (v. 8). They kept the word and had not denied the name of Christ (v. 8). They had persevered (v. 10).

A choice. The faithfulness attributed to this church was a matter of choice. It was not merely that one church had the ability to be great and another did not. The same is true of individuals. It is not that some are just lucky enough to fall into the lot of the faithful. Those who are what they ought to be have made a choice—a decision.

We see in a previous letter that God expects such faithfulness of all (Rev. 2:10). Thus, anyone and any church can make the same choice.

Little strength (v. 8). This was not a condemnation, but a commendation for the use of their little strength. This likely meant that they were not large in number. Obviously, a church doesn't have to be large and growing to be faithful and effective. In fact, some churches become smaller in number because they are faithful to the word. The size of a church, within itself, doesn't tell us whether a church is strong, weak, true or untrue. This church was faithful in spite of its little strength. Today, some small groups think since they are "little," they amount to nothing. This passage tells us that is not so.

This could refer to them having little or no monetary resources.[5] However, having one talent doesn't justify not using the talent we have (Matt. 25:14-30). "Conversely, it is also an encouraging fact to realize that others may regard us as insignificant and unimportant, but the Lord knows even what the 'poor widow' does (Mark 12:41-44; 2 Tim. 2:19)."[6]

---

2   Albert Barnes, *Notes on the New Testament: Revelation*, 92.
3   Homer Hailey, *Revelation, An Introduction and Commentary*, 150.
4   Ray Summers, *Worthy is the Lamb*, 122.
5   If they were small in number, they may have little money. Perhaps both ideas are true.
6   Robert Harkrider, *Revelation*, 51.

Kept my word and not denied my name (v. 8). They were faithful in the service that honors the name of God. They had faced some tests, withstood the forces and yet remained faithful (cf. v. 9). Thus far, they had persevered (v. 10). "When Christians were brought before heathen magistrates in times of persecution, they were required to renounce the name of Christ, and to disown him in a public manner. It is possible that, amidst the persecutions that raged in the early times, the members of the church at Philadelphia had been summoned to such a trial, and they had stood the trial firmly. It would seem from the following verse, that the efforts which had been made to induce them to renounce the name of Christ had been made by those who professed to be Jews, though they evinced the spirit of Satan"[7]

The Encouragement (vv. 8, 9, 11)

Open door (v. 8). An open door is used throughout the Bible to refer to opportunity. There was a "door of faith" open to the Gentiles (Acts 14:27). There was a "great and effective" door open to Paul (1 Cor. 16:9). A door was open to Paul at Troas (2 Cor. 2:12). Paul encouraged the Colossians to pray for a door to be opened to him (Col. 4:3). Thus, the open door is an opportunity, an opening, through which a goal can be accomplished. Likely, this referred to the door of evangelism. As this was a missionary city used to spread the Greek culture, perhaps the circumstances were right for this church to spread the gospel.

Perhaps there are open doors right in front of us that we fail to notice. May we pray that the Lord opens doors of opportunity for us and at the same time gives us wisdom to see and use them.

Your enemy will acknowledge you (v. 9). There were some who claimed to be faithful Jews, but were, because of their compromise, of the synagogue of Satan (cf. 2:9). The Lord promised that those Jews would come and worship before the feet of these saints and know that God loves his people. Obviously, this did not mean they would literally fall down at the feet of Christians and worship. It simply meant they would come to recognize (if not before, then at the judgment) those whom they had opposed as being God's people. The saints would be vindicated. Even though they had to endure persecution, they would ultimately prevail.

Can persevere (v. 11). The Lord encouraged the church saying, "Hold fast what you have, that no one may take your crown." They could persevere. The fact you have persevered (v. 10) is encouragement that you could persevere in the future. It is possible to hold what you have (v. 11). Such perseverance required great determination.

The Promise (vv. 10, 12)

Protection (v. 10). The Lord promised to keep them "from the hour of trial" (v. 10). This is not a promise to keep them from temptation, but keep them from being overwhelmed. The Lord will not allow his people to face a trial greater than they can bear (1 Cor. 10:13). God guards and protects the faithful (1 Pet. 1:5).[8]

Make a pillar in temple (v. 12). The one who overcomes is promised that God will make him a pillar in the temple of God. Obviously that is not literal. "Making one a pillar emphasizes

---

7   Barnes, *ibid.*, 93-94.
8   The word "kept" (NKJV) in this text comes from a military term which means to be guarded or protected (cf. "being guarded", ESV).

the thought of permanence rather than support, as indicated by the assurance, 'and he shall go out thence no more.'"9 Ultimately, it is a promise to dwell in the temple of heaven. The phrase, "and he shall go out no more" may be a contrast to the history of the city of Philadelphia being constantly threatened by earthquakes. The citizens of the city would have to evacuate the city constantly. "The flavor may be: 'If you remain faithful to the truth, you will no more live in fear.'"10

A new name (v. 12). The one who overcomes is promised a new name. Writing on him the name of God would identify him as belonging to God – a child of God. Writing on him the name of the city of God would verify his citizenship in heaven. "The passage is a promise that when Christ makes us completely his own by writing his own new name on us, he will admit us into his full glory, which is at present incomprehensible to us."11

Indeed, it is possible for a church to reach a state that brings no condemnation from the Lord.

Questions

1. How is the Lord (as the author of the letter) identified? _____

2. What does it mean that Christ has the key of David? _____

3. What condemnation is given to this church? _____

4. To what does "little strength" refer to and how would that be a commendation? ____

5. What commendation is given to this church? _____

6. What was the open door this church had? _____

7. In what sense would their enemies worship at their feet? _____

8. In what sense would the Lord keep them from the hour of trial? _____

9. What is the promise of being made a pillar in the temple? _____

10. What point is to be learned from "he shall go out no more."? _____

---

9 Hailey, *ibid.*, 154.
10 Wayne Jackson, *Revelation*, 162.
11 H.D.M. Spence-Jones, *Pulpit Commentary Revelation*, 113.

Revelation 3:14-22
Lesson 9
Letter to the Church at Laodicea
The Church That Was Lukewarm

Outline

I. **Identification of the Author (v. 14)**

II. **Condemnation (vv. 15-19a)**

III. **Plea to Repent (vv. 19b-20)**

IV. **Promise if Overcome (vv. 21-22)**

Key Verses that Summarize the Chapter

Revelation 3:15-16

I know your works, that you are neither cold nor hot. I could wish you were cold or hot. So then, because you are lukewarm, and neither cold nor hot, I will vomit you out of My mouth.

The church at Laodicea received a letter saying you are sickening. You disgust me. You make me want to vomit. The reason? They were lukewarm.

Laodicea was located 40 miles southeast of Philadelphia. The city was known for being rich; so rich, in fact, they needed no help to rebuild after it was mostly destroyed by an earthquake in 60 A.D. "Tacitus, the Roman historian, inferred that it was unusual that any city would be rich enough to rebuild itself (*The Annals of Tacitus*, 14,27.1)."[1]

It was perhaps the main commercial city of the region. This made it an easy target for lethargy and self-satisfied complacency. The commercial background is reflected in this letter (vv. 17-18). Summers lists three main businesses for which the city was known.[2] (1) Laodicia was the banking center for the region. Money was accumulated in this city. Thus, they were rich. (2) There was the black wool market from which they made fine garments. (3) An ointment for the eyes was made and sold here. Thus, they were known for good vision. Residents of Laodicia thought they had true wealth, true raiment and true vision. Yet, as we will see, they were actually in need of true wealth, true raiment and true vision.

---

1 Robert Harkrider, *Revelation*, 55.
2 Ray Summers, *Worthy is the Lamb*, 125-126.

The church at Laodicia was mentioned in the book of Colossians (4:12-16). Laodicia was one of the tri-cities that was in close proximity (Colossae and Hierapolis being the other two). The Colossian letter was to be shared with the church at Laodicia. Likewise, a letter to Laodicia was to be read by the church at Colossae.

The church at Laodicia was the only one of the seven that was all bad. There was no commendation at all.

The Problem (vv. 15-16)

The problem with this church was that they were lukewarm (neither cold nor hot).

They were indifferent. They were plagued with apathy. They were lacking in diligence. The trouble with indifference is that many who have it don't know it. And those who do, don't care.

They were like their own water supply. One of the weaknesses of the city was that it lacked adequate water supply. "Hemer writes that the mineral deposits in the remains of its aqueduct system lend evidence to the theory that its water came from the hot springs to the south. If this is so, the water would have been lukewarm, even after flowing several miles. In contrast, only a few miles away, Colossae had a good supply of refreshing cold water, and Hierapolis prized its hot spring water which helped administer healing to the ailing."[3]

They had knowledge without zeal. This is just the opposite of the Jews (Rom. 10:2). They had zeal without knowledge. They had a general conviction of the truth and the importance of Christianity, but no zeal or enthusiasm about it like many today. They were uncommitted and uninvolved, but had not quit altogether. Church pews are full of such people.

They were neither cold nor hot. If they were hot, they would be diligent and zealous.[4] If they were cold, they would be totally against what is right. One who is cold knows his abject poverty before God. He is honest in the sense there is no disguise or pretense. Obviously, God wants his people to be hot. However, he prefers the honesty of the cold over the pretense of the lukewarm.

This is a spirit with which it is hard to deal. One who is cold is more apt to see the need and change. The lukewarm Christian does not see his need (v. 17). The following is a picture of a lukewarm Christian.[5]

- He loves God, but just not first.
- He believes that religion is a good and important thing to have in life, but thinks it should not consume him.
- He loves others in theory, but in practice does very little for strangers and the outcast.
- He has good intentions to participate in good deeds someday, but doesn't redeem his time and resources to take action.

---

3   Harkrider, *ibid.*, 56-57.
4   The word "hot" in our text is from the root word for zeal or zealous. "Late verbal from [zeô], to boil, (Rom. 12:11), boiling hot, here only in N. T." (A. T. Robertson, *Word Pictures of the New Testament*, (Rev. 3:15).
5   This list is taken from Phillip Shumake, *Lifelong Zeal*, 21-22.

- He loves hearing stories about those who live zealously for God, but the stories never inspire real change and greater zeal in his own life.
- He is often silent about his faith.
- He settles into a one sided religion (personal or doctrinal).
- He leans on his own strength rather than full faith in God.

Indeed, it is hard to see what we are not doing. Overt acts of sin are easily seen by self and others (i.e. lying, cheating, stealing, drinking, or cursing). Even sins of attitude that involve doing are easily seen (i.e. hate, lust, bitterness, envy, jealousy, and anger). It is harder to detect what I fail to do. It is even harder to see that I don't care as much as I should, that I'm not as involved as I should be, that I am not dedicated as I ought to be, or that I should have grown more by now. This is especially true with one whose apathy has not caused him to quit altogether.

The Reason (v. 17)

This church was lukewarm because they didn't see themselves as they really were. "Because you say, 'I am rich, have become wealthy, and have need of nothing'—and do not know that you are wretched, miserable, poor, blind, and naked" (Rev. 3:17).

They had a false sense of security. They viewed themselves as in need of nothing (v. 17). They reasoned they were self-sufficient since they were rich. Since they thought they were doing quite well, there was no need to be concerned about the spiritual.

"You say" (v. 17) *suggests that in their own eyes they viewed themselves to be strong.* "Like many modern Christians who do just enough to keep their names on a church roll, they would likely have been insulted had anyone else accused them of being lukewarm and unpleasing before the Lord."[6]

They didn't see their real condition (v. 17). In actuality they were wretched (deplorable), miserable (to be pitied), poor (in real need), blind (can't see), and naked (lacking so much). They were just the opposite of what they thought.

They were calloused. Much like the picture of the apostate that the Hebrew writer gives, they were no longer pricked or moved by the word (Heb. 6:4-6). It is altogether possible to allow the word to become meaningless. The more we hear it preached and taught and are not moved by it at all (remaining lukewarm), it then becomes meaningless.

The Reaction (vv. 16, 19, 20)

By reaction, we mean God's reaction. God was greatly displeased with this church.

Spew them out (v. 16). The ESV says "I will spit you out of my mouth." The NKJV renders this, "I will vomit you out of My mouth." In other words, they made God sick. God is disgusted with indifference. This is a statement of God's utter rejection of them in their lukewarm state. This is the Lord's view of carelessness, indifference and slothfulness.

---

6   Harkrider, *ibid.*, 59.

Rebukes and chastens (v. 19). God rebukes and chastens because of his love and concern. His rebuke of them is not out of being inconsiderate as some would view a rebuke today. God disciplines as a father would a child.

Knocks and pleads (v. 20). God is pictured as standing at the door knocking, desiring to come into their dwelling. He will not force himself. He waits for admission. Those who are lukewarm are not answering the door. "Intimating that, though they had erred, the way of repentance and hope was not closed against them. He was still willing to be gracious, though their conduct had been such as to be loathsome, ver. 16. To see the real force of this language, we must remember how disgusting and offensive their conduct had been to him. And yet he was willing, notwithstanding this, to receive them to his favour; nay more, he stood and pled with them that he might be received with the hospitality that would be shown to a friend or stranger."[7]

The Answer (vv. 18-19)

The only answer to the lukewarm heart is repentance.

Buy from me (v. 18). While they thought there was no need, they were indeed lacking. They needed to buy gold (spiritual gold) from God so they would be rich. They needed to buy a white garment (spiritual garment) so they would be clothed. They needed to buy eye salve (spiritual salve) so they could see. This is often the case today. Because we have possessions, clothes, and medical care, we think we are just fine. Yet, we may be lacking (spiritually) in all of those areas.

To buy these from God simply means to do what has to be done to attain them – whatever effort or sacrifice may be necessary.

Be zealous (v. 19). This is the opposite of being lukewarm. To be zealous is to be hot.[8] Since this is commanded, it can be done. Furthermore, we can just do it rather than struggle with knowing how. Any service to the Lord needs to be given life and vitality (cf. Col. 3:23).

Repent (v. 19). Repentance is a change of mind resulting in a change of life. When the lukewarm repent, they start doing what they are failing to do. There is a direct connection between being zealous and repenting. Barnes observes, "Be earnest, strenuous, ardent in your purpose to exercise true repentance, and to turn from the error of your ways. Lose no time; spare no labour, that you may obtain such a state of mind that it shall not be necessary to bring upon you the severe discipline which always comes on those who continue lukewarm in religion. The *truth* taught here is, that when the professed followers of Christ have become lukewarm in his service, they should lose no time in returning to him, and seeking his favour again. As sure as he has any true love for them, if this is not done he will bring upon them some heavy calamity, alike to rebuke them for their errors, and to recover them to himself."[9]

A lukewarm church cannot continue in that state. A change is demanded.

---

7   Albert Barnes, *Notes on the New Testament: Revelation*, 103.
8   The word zealous (v. 19) is kin to the word hot (v. 16) (M. R. Vincent, *Word Studies in the New Testament,* 2:473).
9   *Ibid.,* 103.

Questions

1. What three businesses were notable in Laodicia? _____
   _____
   _____

2. What does it mean to be lukewarm? _____
   _____

3. Why is it hard to deal with the lukewarm heart? _____
   _____

4. What gave this church a false sense of security? _____
   _____

5. How did God react to this church's lukewarm spirit? _____
   _____

6. What practical point do we learn from the connection between love and rebuke (v. 19)? _____
   _____
   _____

7. How does one buy gold, a white garment and salve from God? _____
   _____
   _____

8. How does one overcome a lukewarm heart? _____
   _____
   _____

9. What is the connection between zeal and repentance (v. 19)? _____
   _____
   _____

10. What has impressed you most about the letters to the seven churches? _____
    _____
    _____
    _____

Revelation 4-5

Lesson 10
The Throne Scene

Chapter 4
God is on His Throne – In Control

Outline

I. God on His Throne (vv. 1-3)

   A. *John was taken in a vision to see One on the throne (vv. 1-2)*
   B. *Description of One on the throne (v. 3)*
      1. Like jasper and sardius in appearance
      2. Rainbow around the throne
      3. Appearance like an emerald

II. What Was Around the Throne (vv. 4-8a)

   A. *Twenty-four elders (v. 4)*
      1. Clothed in white robes
      2. Crown on head
   B. *Surroundings (vv. 5-6a)*
      1. Lightnings (v. 5)
      2. Thunderings (v. 5)
      3. Voices (v. 5)
      4. Seven lamps (seven spirits) (v. 5)
      5. Sea of glass (v. 6a)
   C. *Four living creatures (vv. 6b-8a)*
      1. Like a lion, calf, face of man and flying eagle (v. 6b-7)
      2. Six wings each (v. 8a)
      3. Full of eyes (v. 6b)

III. Worship Before the Throne (vv. 8b-11)

   A. *Holy (v. 8)*
   B. *Almighty (vv. 8, 11)*
   C. *Eternal (vv. 8, 9, 10)*
   D. *Created all for his will (v. 11)*

Key Verse that Summarizes the Chapter

Revelation 4:2

Immediately I was in the Spirit; and behold, a throne set in heaven, and One sat on the throne.

With this chapter we begin the apocalyptic portion of the book. A door is open and we are allowed, through John's eyes, to access the throne of God. Chapter 4 focuses on the Father. The next chapter focuses on Christ, the Son.

God on His Throne (vv. 1-3)

John was taken in a vision to see One on the throne (vv. 1-2). John saw a door standing open and a voice, like a trumpet (the voice of one in authority), invited him to come in before the throne. The voice told John he would be shown "things that must take place after this" (v. 1). Being allowed to see things from God's point of view, he would be shown what will shortly take place in the conflict with Domitian.

John was taken in a vision ("in the Spirit", v. 2)[1] into heaven where he saw a throne and God sitting on the throne (v. 2). Here we are introduced to the major point of these two chapters (if not the whole book): **God is still on his throne and in control**. While it looked (from the viewpoint on earth) like Domitian had the upper hand and all was lost for those striving to follow Christ, John and the saints in Asia were reminded that God is still on his throne and in control.

Description of One on the throne (v. 3). The depiction here is one in authority that has glory and honor. The appearance is like a jasper stone which is clear as crystal (Rev. 21:11), suggesting purity, holiness and righteousness. The sardius stone "denotes a precious stone of a blood-red, or sometimes of a flesh-colour, more commonly known by the name of carnelian."[2] This may suggest divine justice. The rainbow is a reminder of God's judgment and mercy. It is a symbol of hope. The vision of God on his throne is designed to give hope to John and his readers.

What Was Around the Throne (vv. 4-8a)

Twenty-four elders (v. 4). The twenty-four may be two groups of twelve. Under the Old Testament there were twelve tribes. Under the New Testament there were twelve apostles. Perhaps this refers to the combined redeemed gathered around the throne. The white garments suggest purity. The crowns indicate victory.

Surroundings (vv. 5-6a). The lightnings, thunderings, and voices seem to be symbols of authority and power. The seven spirits most likely refer to the Holy Spirit. Seven would indicate the completeness of his work. The seven lamps may refer to the Spirit's work of illumination. Whatever the case, the point of the surroundings is to emphasize the power and authority of God. In light of the first four seals (chapter 6), they display a manifestation of God's wrath. God is displeased with what Rome is doing to his people.

The sea of glass, clear as crystal (symbolizing purity), that was before the throne shows that the throne of the exalted God is unapproachable, at least for the present.[3] Yet, later we see a time when there is no more sea (Rev. 21:1).

---

1   Compare Revelation 1:10.
2   Albert Barnes, *Notes on the New Testament: Revelation*, 109.
3   John was able to approach it only in a vision.

Four living creatures (vv. 6b-8a). Around the throne were four living creatures. Here we are reminded of a similar scene in Ezekiel (1:10; 10:20-22).[4] One was like a lion, one like a calf, one like a man, and the last like a flying eagle. Summers suggest, "they represent the fourfold division of animal life so that all God's creatures are worshiping him. The lion represents wild animal life, the calf represents domestic animal life, the man represents human life, and the eagle represents bird life. All are represented as constantly watchful to adore and worship God. The whole creation – man, beast and bird – is pictured as glorified with him as part of his sovereignty."[5]

The creatures have six wings each. This is very much like Isaiah 6:2 where the seraphim have six wings each. With two he covered his face or eyes (humility), with two he covered his feet (modesty), and with two he flew (eager to serve). The four creatures are full of eyes suggesting that they are able to see completely and fully the one on the throne. Thus, what they say about the one on the throne is absolutely true.

Whatever these four living creatures represent, the point is that they are praising God as one who is holy and in control of all. Don't lose sight of the point of the chapter: *God is on his throne and in control.*

Worship Before the Throne (vv. 8b-11)

Here we see the four living creatures and the twenty-four elders praising God.

Holy (v. 8). "The repetition of a name, or of an expression, three times, was quite common among the Jews."[6] The footnote in the NKJV says that "M" (Majority text) has "holy" nine times (a multiple of three). God is praised for his holiness and purity.

Almighty (vv. 8, 11). God is the all-powerful God, as evidenced in the fact he created all things (v. 11). Thus, God is in control of all.

Eternal (vv. 8, 9, 10). God is praised as the one who was, is and is to come (v. 8). He lives forever (vv. 9-10). In contrast to the Roman Emperor who lives but a short life span, God lives forever and ever. He thus rules over the kings and emperors of the earth.

Created all for his will (v. 11). Since God created all things, he must be in control of all things. In fact, by his will, "they exist and were created." The world was created to be used for God's purpose. God created a world that he could control, and thus use for his purpose. Here is one of the greatest statements of the providence of God.

Homer Hailey gave this illustration many years ago: A car is built upon certain laws or principles. The laws state that if you turn the steering wheel to the right, the car goes to the right. If you turn it to the left, it goes left. If you press on the accelerator it goes faster. If you press on the brake, it slows down and stops. If you put it in drive it goes forward. If you put it in reverse, it goes backwards. When you sit in the driver's seat you control the car, yet within the confines of the laws upon which it was built. In the universe, God is in

---

4   In Ezekiel the four faces seem to represent the following: man (intelligence), lion (strength), ox or calf (service), and eagle (swiftness).
5   *ibid.*, 133.
6   Albert Barnes, *Notes on the Old Testament: Isaiah*, 1:139.

the driver's seat. He is steering this world where he wants. He can and is doing so without violating the natural laws upon which it was built. That is how providence works.

Since the world exists for God's purpose, he is in control of it all, even though it seems like Domitian and his cohorts have the upper hand.

Revelation 5
Worthy is the Lamb & the Scroll

Outline

I. A Scroll That No One Could Open (vv. 1-4)

  A. *Scroll with seven seals (v. 1)*
  B. *No one found worthy to open the seals (vv. 2-4)*

II. The Lamb Takes the Scroll (vv. 5-7)

  A. *The Lion (v. 5)*
  B. *The Lamb (vv. 6-7)*

III. Worship of the Lamb as Worthy (vv. 8-14)

  A. *By four living creatures and the twenty-four elders (vv. 8-10)*
  B. *By many angels (vv. 11-12)*
  C. *By every creature (vv. 13-14)*

Key Verse that Summarizes the Chapter

Revelation 5:12

Saying with a loud voice: "Worthy is the Lamb who was slain to receive power and riches and wisdom and strength and honor and glory and blessing!"

This chapter is a continuation of the throne scene of chapter 4. The previous chapter focuses on Jehovah God who sits on the throne. Here the focus is on Christ, the worthy lamb who becomes the central figure in the book. Some have suggested that these two chapters could be summarized in the words of the Lord himself, "you believe in God [chapter 4], believe also in Me" [chapter 5] (John 14:1). As the reader considers the power of God (chapter 4), he is urged to look to the love of the redeeming lamb of God (chapter 5) as a source of comfort and consolation.

A Scroll That No One Could Open (vv. 1-4)

Scroll with seven seals (v. 1). John looked and saw a scroll in the right hand of God as he sat on the throne. It was written to capacity (on the inside and on the back). It was complete, lacking nothing. It was completely sealed with seven seals. The message was hidden until the seven seals were opened.

What was the message in the scroll? It would reveal the future of God's people and their struggle. It touched on God's eternal purpose (cf. v. 9). We will see the contents of the scroll in chapters 6-11.

No one found worthy to open the seals (vv. 2-4). John heard a strong[7] angel ask, "Who is worthy to open the scroll and to loose its seals?" (v. 2). "That is, who is 'worthy' in the sense of having a rank so exalted, and attributes so comprehensive, as to authorize and enable him to do it. In other words, who has the requisite endowments of all kinds to enable him to do it? It would require moral qualities of an exalted character to justify him in approaching the seat of the holy God, to take the book from his hands; it would require an ability beyond that of any created being to penetrate the future, and disclose the meaning of the symbols which were employed."[8]

At first, no one in heaven or on earth could be found worthy to open the scroll. It seemed to John that he would never know what he had hoped to see (cf. 4:1). So he wept.

The Lamb Takes the Scroll (vv. 5-7)

The Lion (v. 5). One of the elders told John not to weep for one had been found to open the scroll. The book (scroll) was a means of introducing the reader to the Christ, the central figure in the book. The elder directed John's attention to the Lion of the tribe of Judah. This alludes to Judah being called a "lion's whelp" and the promise that the scepter would not depart from Judah (Gen. 49:9-10). Thus, the Messiah is out of Judah and has the authority and the strength of a lion.

The Lion is said to be "the Root of David." This is more than the descendant (offspring) of David. He is David's source.[9]

The Lion has "prevailed."[10] "The tense indicates that the event has already been achieved. The victory was won at Calvary – the rest is a mopping-up campaign!"[11]

The Lamb (vv. 6-7). When John turned to see the Lion, he saw a Lamb. Though the Lamb had been slain (the atoning sacrifice, John 1:29), he now stands (overcame in the resurrection and is thus victorious). The seven horns may suggest his omnipotence. The seven eyes may point to his omniscience.

The Lamb came and took the scroll from the right hand of God (v. 7). Summers contends that the aorist tense pictures "the whole action in one flash…It shows an unhesitant attitude and a spirit of strong determination on the part of the Lamb as 'the first thing you know

---

7   "Either as being of higher rank, or with reference to the great voice." (M. R. Vincent, *Word studies in the New Testament*, 2:488).
8   Albert Barnes, *Notes on the New Testament: Revelation*, 122.
9   See Wayne Jackson, *Revelation*, 43. Also see Robert Harkrider, *Revelation*, 72. Compare Matthew 22:42-45.
10 "Conquered", ESV; "overcome", ASV; "triumphed", NIV; "has won the victory", NCV.
11 Jackson, *ibid.*, 43.

he has taken the book right out of the hand of him who sat on the throne.' Only Christ can open the book and carry forward God's judgments on wicked men. The destiny of men is in the nail-pierced hands of the Lamb who was slain."[12]

Worship of the Lamb as Worthy (vv. 8-14)

The rest of this chapter is devoted to the praise John witnessed showing that indeed the Lamb is worthy to take the scroll.

By four living creatures and the twenty-four elders (vv. 8-10). The four living creatures and the twenty-four elders bow down before the Lamb. Each has a harp (used for praise). Each of them has golden bowls of incense (which were the prayers of the saints). The point to be learned is that God is listening. Their prayers are heard!

They sang a new song (not new in time, but new in kind). The song focused on the redemptive work of Christ (vv. 9-10). It is new in that there is nothing else like it or experienced before. Notice these four things about the redemption through Christ:[13]

  1. It is for God (v. 9). We are redeemed "to God." We have first been saved for God's own use.

  2. It is by the blood of Christ. Our redemption is only possible by the sacrifice of the blood of the Lamb (Eph. 1:7; Col. 1:14).

  3. It is unlimited. Redemption is available to all—to every tribe, tongue, people and nation.

  4. It made us a kingdom. By the redemptive work of the Lamb we have been made a kingdom of priest (Exo. 19:6). We have been made kings to serve as priests.

By many angels (vv. 11-12). Next John sees the multitude of angels praising the Lamb for his power (authority), riches (which are unsearchable), wisdom (from the mind of God & because he is God), strength (power over all), and his glory (worthy of all praise and honor).

By every creature (vv. 13-14). The last scene is that every creature praised both the Father who sits on the throne and the Lamb who lives forever and ever.

In this chapter we are introduced to the Lamb of God (the central figure in the book). He is praised for being worthy (v. 12), the Lion (vv. 5-6), the Lamb (v. 6), all powerful (v. 6), all knowing (v. 6), eternal (v. 14), and the one who redeemed us (vv. 8-9).

"Believing in the power of God (chap. 4) and the redeeming love of God (chap. 5), there is no enemy or force of evil which Christians need to fear. They can enter the conflict or endure evil knowing that God is still on his throne; he has not laid aside his scepter; he has not abandoned his throne to any other. He is mightier than all the forces arrayed against his people. Faith in him gives man the proper evaluation of life, of its issues and their outcome."[14]

---

12 Summers, *ibid.*, 136.
13 These four points are taken from Summers, *ibid.*, 136-137.
14 Summers, *ibid.*, 137.

Questions

1. What is the main point to be learned from chapter four? _____
   _____
   _____

2. Who or what is represented by the twenty-four elders? _____
   _____

3. What is the significance of the sea of glass and what do we learn about it later in the book? _____
   _____

4. What comfort would the reader get from the statement that God is the Almighty (4:8, 11)? _____
   _____

5. What do we learn about the providence of God from 4:11? _____
   _____
   _____

6. What do we know about the content or message of the scroll mentioned in chapter 5? _____
   _____

7. Why would the Christ be called a Lion? _____
   _____

8. Why would the Christ be called a Lamb? _____
   _____

9. What important lesson would the reader gain from the golden bowls of incense? __
   _____
   _____

10. What is meant that our redemption is "for God" (5:9)? _____
    _____
    _____

Revelation 6

Lesson 11
Opening of the Six Seals

Outline

I. First Seal – White Horse & Rider (Victory) (vv. 1-2)

II. Second Seal – Red Horse & Rider (War) (vv. 3-4)

III. Third Seal – Black Horse & Rider (Famine) (vv. 5-6)

IV. Fourth Seal – Pale Horse & Rider (Death) (vv. 7-8)

V. Fifth Seal – Souls Under the Altar (Persecution) (vv. 9-10)

VI. Sixth Seal – Shakeup of Nature (Judgment) (vv. 12-17)

> **Key Verse that Summarizes the Chapter**
>
> **Revelation 6:1**
>
> Now I saw when the Lamb opened one of the seals; and I heard one of the four living creatures saying with a voice like thunder, "Come and see."

This chapter begins the opening of the seals on the scroll. Six of the seven are revealed in this chapter.

"The main action of the book of Revelation begins with this vision. The remainder of Revelation is in reality an explanation of the seals of the little book of destiny. Back of all history is God in Christ; in this book we see the hand of Christ opening the sealed book of God's dealings with men."[1]

The first four seals go together. The horses and riders are all going in the same direction.[2] They point to the overthrow of Rome. The fifth seal points to the cause for the overthrow, while the sixth points to the judgment of God upon Rome.

There is little or no question about the fifth and sixth seal. However, there are different schools of thought on the first four. Some think they are pointing to Christ and his victory through the spread of the gospel. Others think they point to the temporary victory that Rome experiences. It seems to make more sense that the first four deal with the overthrow

---
1 Ray Summers, *Worthy is the Lamb*, 139.
2 The four living creatures, as they announce the opening of the first four seals, seem to tie them together.

of Rome. Keep in mind that whatever these are about they involve things that would "shortly take place" (1:1) and "things that must shortly take place after this" (4:1).[3]

First Seal—White Horse & Rider (Victory) (vv. 1-2)

John was invited by one of the four living creatures to "come and see." When he looked he saw a white horse and a rider with a bow and crown. He was going out to conquer.

White is the color of victory. A bow is an instrument of war. The crown is worn in victory. Thus, we have a scene of conquering and victory. Rome will be conquered. There will be an outside conquest upon Rome. Summers contends, "The horseman is not a Roman but a Parthian cavalryman – the most dreaded enemy that Rome had. The Roman warriors did not use a bow; however, it was the favorite weapon of the Parthians."[4]

Let us not get bogged down in every detail of the imagery in this or the rest of the book. Let's focus on the summary point of each one. Perhaps the following sums up the first seal best: "Thus is pictured to the Christians that victory is coming. Mighty Rome is not always to stand. Outside conquest will be a part of the method of her destruction. God held in his hand the means of deliverance for his people."[5]

Second Seal—Red Horse & Rider (War) (vv. 3-4)

The apostle was again invited by another of the four creatures to come and see. This time, he saw a fiery red horse whose rider had the mission of taking peace from the earth. When that was accomplished, people would kill one another. This rider was given a great sword.

Red is the color of conflict and war. It seems only natural that the red horse (bloody means of carrying out the victory) would follow close behind the white horse. The statement, "that people should kill one another" (v. 4) may suggest that in the middle of such conflict anarchy reigns.

Third Seal—Black Horse & Rider (Famine) (vv. 5-6)

A third creature invited John to come and see. This time he saw a black horse whose rider had a pair of scales in his hand. As this horse passed by a voice said, "A quart of wheat for a denarius, and three quarts of barley for a denarius; and do not harm the oil and the wine" (v. 6).

Black is the color of darkness, gloom, and depression. The scales and the price of wheat and barley suggest some form of rationing. The cost mentioned by the voice is 10-12 times higher than normal.[6] Thus, considering the black color, famine seems to be the picture. "Famine always follows in the wake of war."[7] Though the necessities are scarce and sky high, the luxuries (oil and wine) are abundant.

---

3   We cannot afford to be dogmatic on the interpretation of these seals. The differences we are discussing here is not between truth and error (i.e. Premillennialism), but that of interpretations, anyone of which would be hard to prove.
4   ibid., 140.
5   Summers, ibid., 140.
6   A denarius was "about 1 day's wage for a worker" (NKJV footnote).
7   Summers, ibid., 141.

Fourth Seal—Pale Horse & Rider (Death) (vv. 7-8)

The final living creature called for John to come and see. This time he saw a pale horse. The rider's name was Death. Hades followed with him. This rider was given power over a fourth of the earth to kill by means of a sword, hunger, death, and beast.

The name of the rider tells us the significance of the pale color as well as his mission. "All of the above – military conquest, war, famine, pestilence – are forces God can use to destroy the oppressors of his people. His Christians are to take courage. Their cause is not lost by any means."[8]

The power over a fourth of the earth shows that the destruction is not complete. Rome will be overthrown, but this is not utter destruction.

Fifth Seal—Souls Under the Altar (Persecution) (vv. 9-10)

The seals are no longer being announced by one of the four living creatures. When this one was opened, John saw souls under the altar who had been slain for the word of God. They cried out with a loud voice asking how long until God would avenge their blood. They were then given a white robe and told to rest a little while until their number was completed.

Here the focus is on the reason for the overthrow of Rome (described in the first four seals): the persecution of God's people. Just as the blood of the animals offered on the altar in the Old Testament flowed underneath the altar, so here the souls of those who were killed in the persecution were under the altar.

These were slain "for the word of God" (v. 9). Just as John was on Patmos "for the word of God" (1:9), they were killed because of their allegiance to God and his word.[9] Their cry was a plea for justice for what had been done to the people of God.

In response, they were given white robes showing their victory. God has not forgotten his people who have been slain. God will vindicate his people. Until then, they are told to "rest a little while longer" (v. 11). That is, be patient for in time God will take care of things. There are others who will be killed like them before it is over (v. 11).

"This paragraph reflects the moral necessity for judgment. God could not be a righteous God and allow such evil to go unavenged. The chief reason for God's judgment on the Roman Empire was their persecution of God's people...Each one of them was given a white robe, symbolical of their victory and purity, and they were told to be patient. The time was not ripe for God's retribution; there were others in the churches who were to suffer, but in the end certain victory would be realized; judgment was on its way."[10]

---

8   Summers, *ibid.*, 142.
9   The "testimony which they held" may refer to being faithful to their claims.
10 Summers, *ibid.*, 142-143.

Sixth Seal – Shakeup of Nature (Judgment) (vv. 12-17)

When the sixth seal was opened, there was an earthquake, the sun turned black, the moon became like blood, and the stars fell to the earth. The sky then opened as a scroll and every mountain and island was moved. Everyone from kings to slaves hid themselves in caves and in the rocks of the mountains crying out for the rocks and mountains to fall on them and hide them from the wrath of the Lamb.

There is little question that the expressions used here refer to judgment (not the final judgment) upon Rome. These were used in the Old Testament in describing either God's punishment upon or the downfall of some nation. The earthquake (v. 12) is used of God's punishment upon Judah (Isa. 29:6). The sun being darkened and the moon turning to blood are found in God's judgment upon Babylon (Isa. 13:10), Judah (Joel 2:10), and other nations (Joel 3:15). The stars falling, like that of the sun and moon being darkened, describes the overthrow and upheaval of a nation and its leaders (cf. Ezek. 32:7-8; Joel 2:31; Amos 5:18; Matt. 24:29).

So what is the point of this chapter? When the first four seals are unleashed, this is what will happen to Rome. This is the wrath of the Lamb (v. 16). "Under any condition this part of the pageant symbolizes God's destructive power against those who reject him and his plan of salvation. As these forces - conquest, war, famine, pestilence, natural calamity – rage, 'who shall be able to stand?'"[11] The answer to the question of who is able to stand (v. 17) is found in the next chapter.

Questions

1. How does Rev. 1:1 and 4:1 help in understanding what these seals represent? _____
   _____
   _____

2. What tells us that the first four seals are threaded together (i.e. they are going in the same direction? _____
   _____

3. What is the first seal and what does it represent? _____
   _____
   _____

4. What is the second seal and what does it represent? _____
   _____
   _____

5. What is the third seal and what does it represent? _____
   _____
   _____

---

11 Summers, *ibid.*, 145.

6. What is the fourth seal and what does it represent? _____
_____
_____

7. What is the fifth seal and what does it represent? _____
_____
_____

8. What is the sixth seal and what does it represent? _____
_____
_____

9. What does "for the word of God" (v. 9) mean? _____
_____
_____

10. How do we know the sun being darkened, the moon turning to blood and the stars falling are not to be taken literal? _____
_____
_____

Revelation 7

Lesson 12
An Interlude: The Sealing of God's People

Outline

I. **Sealing of 144,000 (vv. 1-8)**

   A. *No harm done till God's people are sealed (vv. 1-3)*
      1. Four angels (given power to harm the earth) restrained (v. 1)
      2. Angel with the seal cries "do no harm till we have sealed" God's people (vv. 2-3)

   B. *Number was 144,000 (vv. 4-8)*

II. **The Great Multitude Around the Throne (vv. 9-17)**

   A. *Worship God (vv. 9-12)*
      1. Cry "Salvation belongs to God..." (vv. 9-10)
      2. Worship with angels, elders and four living creatures (vv. 11-12)

   B. *Washed their robes in the blood of the Lamb (vv. 13-14)*

   C. *With God and the Lamb (vv. 15-17)*
      1. They serve God before the throne and God dwells with them (v. 15)
      2. Lamb shepherds them (vv. 16-17)
         a. Hunger no more (v. 16)
         b. Suffer heat/sun no more (v. 16)
         c. Led to living waters (v. 17)
         d. Tears wiped away (v. 17)

Key Verse that Summarizes the Chapter

Revelation 7:3

Saying, "Do not harm the earth, the sea, or the trees till we have sealed the servants of our God on their foreheads."

We label chapter seven an interlude for the writer pauses between the opening of the sixth and seventh seals to answer the question raised at the end of the previous chapter. The question was, "For the great day of His wrath has come, and who is able to stand?" (Rev. 6:17). Who will escape the wrath of God? The answer is God's people. What will happen to the people of God while this destructive work takes place? The answer is that they will be protected by God. So, chapter seven answers that question.

Sealing of 144,000 (vv. 1-8)

No harm done till God's people are sealed (vv. 1-3). The scene opens with four angels restraining the destructive forces until God's people could be sealed. They are pictured as holding back the wind. The Old Testament uses wind to depict God's judgment upon a nation (cf. Jer. 4:11-12; 18:17; 49:32, 36; Ezek. 5:2; 12:14; Isa. 41:16). Thus, restraining the wind is holding back the destructive judgment of God until God has sealed his people.

The sealing refers to marking or identifying God's people (cf. Ezek. 9:1-7; 2 Tim. 2:19). Here (in light of restraining the destructive forces) it is used as a symbol of protection. Those who are marked or sealed are God's people who will stand.

Number was 144,000 (vv. 4-8). The number here is not literal.[1] The seal or mark on the forehead (v. 3) is not literal. The four corners of the earth (v. 1) are not literal. The 144,000 are from the twelve tribes (v. 8). Thus, if this is literal language, a Gentile could not be included. If this only includes the literal twelve tribes, that mean would that Abraham, Isaac, and Jacob would not be included since they were never of the twelve tribes.[2] If this is a literal number, then there could not be 144,001.

This number suggests the idea of completeness. It is a multiple of 12 (the religious number) multiplied by 1000. There were 12,000 from each of the twelve tribes (vv. 5-8).[3] Thus, absolute completeness. Not one of the faithful will be lost.

The Great Multitude Around the Throne (vv. 9-17)

What is the contrast between those mentioned in verses 1-8 and those in verses 9-17? Some think it is a contrast between Jews (vv. 1-8) and Gentiles (vv. 9-17). However, the Jew versus Gentile distinction is not drawn elsewhere in the book of Revelation. If this is the contrast, why was the restraint universal (v. 1)? Would this mean that the Gentiles were not sealed since nothing is said in verses 9-17 about sealing? The 144,00 are mentioned again in Revelation 14:1 where it refers to all the redeemed. At the end of the book all of God's people are sealed (22:4). Thus, we have to conclude that those in verses 1-8 are the same people as in verses 9-17. The difference seems to be that the first eight verses are a picture of God's people now, whereas the next nine are a snapshot of the same people in heaven.[4] These are two pictures of the same people.

Worship God (vv. 9-12). John then looked and saw a great multitude standing before the throne and the Lamb. They were clothed in white robes (representing purity and victory). The palm branches (perhaps alluding to their use in celebration of the Feast of Tabernacles, (Lev. 23:40)[5] gives us an image of festive celebration.

---

1 The Jehovah's Witnesses try to make this number literal.
2 See Wayne Jackson, *Revelation: Jesus Christ's Final Message of Hope*, 57.
3 The 144,000 is spiritual Israel (Jas. 1:1; 1 Pet. 1:1; Gal. 6:6; Phil. 3:3, etc).
4 The Jehovah's Witnesses believe that the great multitude represents the "earth class" who will live on earth forever. However, this multitude is standing before the throne in heaven (v. 15; cf. 11:19). See Jackson, ibid., 175.
5 Compare also John 12:13.

The multitude shouted out praise saying "salvation belongs to our God who sits on the throne, and to the Lamb" (vv. 9-10). Salvation is probably used here in the sense of the victory in overcoming with the Lamb (Rev. 17:14).

The angels, elders and four living creatures fell prostrate before the throne praising God for his wisdom, power and might (vv. 11-12). Only through God was the victory possible. This encouraged the reader to put his trust and confidence in the Almighty God.

Washed their robes in blood of the Lamb (vv. 13-14). Here the great multitude is identified. One of the elders asked John if he knew who these were in the white robes, and from where they were. John said, "Sir, you know" (v. 14). "The simple meaning of the phrase 'thou knowest' is, that he who had asked the question must be better informed than he to whom he had proposed it. It is, on the part of John, a modest confession that he did not know, or could not be presumed to know, and at the same time the respectful utterance of an opinion that he who addressed this question to him must be in possession of this knowledge."[6]

The elder identified them as those who came out of the great tribulation (i.e. the ones who had suffered the great persecution on earth).[7] They now stand before the throne in white robes that have been washed and made white by the blood of the Lamb (v. 14). These are the redeemed who remained faithful when the pressure from Rome was on them.[8]

With God and the Lamb (vv. 15-17). The closing scene of the chapter is that of the multitude dwelling with God serving him continually (v. 15). With the Lamb of God in the midst of the throne he will shepherd them by providing their needs (leading them to living waters; no hunger or thirsting anymore), protecting them (no sun or heat anymore) and removing their problems (wiping away their tears).

So, what is the point of this chapter? God's people will escape the wrath of the Lamb. "Review the relation in which the two divisions of the chapter stand. The persons referred to are the same; their positions in the two divisions differ. In one they are sealed and safe as judgment rains down upon the earth. They are under God's protection and are delivered not from it but through it. In the second division, they are seen after they have come through the difficulties. They possess peace, joy, victory. Every want is supplied; every sorrow healed; every tear wiped away. They are sealed on earth; they wear victorious robes and carry joyous palm branches as they worship around the throne of God in heaven. The two visions together give the most complete picture of the security of God's people before the judgments pictured in chapters 6 and 8. 'Who is able to stand?' Here is the answer."[9]

---

6   Albert Barnes, *Notes on the New Testament: Revelation*, 185.
7   "There is utterly no evidence that the expression denotes a specific seven-year Tribulation Period, as advocated by premillennial dispensationalists" (Wayne Jackson, *ibid.*, 176).
8   These seem to be the same ones who were the souls under the altar (Rev. 6:9-11).
9   Ray Summers, *Worthy is the Lamb*, 152-153.

Questions

1. What is the question that is being answered in this chapter? _____
   _____

2. How is the wind used in this chapter? _____
   _____

3. What does it mean that the people of God were sealed? _____
   _____

4. How do we know that the 144,000 is not to be taken as a literal number? _____
   _____
   _____

5. If the 144,000 is not literal, why is the number used? _____
   _____
   _____

6. What is the contrast between verses 1-8 and verses 9-17? _____
   _____
   _____

7. How do we know that the contrast is not between Jews (vv. 1-8) and Gentiles (vv. 9-17)?
   _____
   _____
   _____

8. How does the elder identify the great multitude? _____
   _____

9. What does this chapter say to those who are enduring persecution? _____
   _____
   _____

10. What is the point of this chapter? _____
    _____
    _____

Revelation 8

Lesson 13
Opening of the Seventh Seal: Four of the Seven Trumpets

Outline

I. **Opening of the Seventh Seal (vv. 1-6)**

   A. *Silence in heaven for one half hour* (v. 1)

   B. *Seven angels prepare to sound their trumpets* (vv. 2, 6)

   C. *Another angel at the altar* (vv. 3-5)
      1. Offers incense with prayers of the saints (vv. 3-4)
      2. Took fire and threw it to the earth (v. 5)

II. **Four Trumpets Sounded (vv. 7-12)**

   A. *First trumpet—Plant life burned up* (v. 7)

   B. *Second trumpet—Sea creatures and ships destroyed* (vv. 8-9)

   C. *Third trumpet—Waters became wormwood* (vv. 10-11)

   D. *Fourth trumpet—Sun, moon, and stars darkened* (v. 12)

III. **Eagle Flying – Announces Woes from Remaining Trumpets (v. 13)**

Key Verse that Summarizes the Chapter

Revelation 8:1

When He opened the seventh seal, there was silence in heaven for about half an hour.

With this chapter we continue the opening of the seven seals out of which comes seven trumpets. Four of the seven trumpets are found in this chapter.

Opening of the Seventh Seal (vv. 1-6)

Silence in heaven for one half hour (v. 1). The long period of silence may suggest a delay in judgment similar to the restraining of the winds (cf. 7:1-3). Or it could be given for the dramatic effect of waiting in breathless silence to see what is revealed in this last seal. "It is not at all improbable that both ideas are here symbolized—dramatic expectation as judgment is delayed."[1]

Seven angels prepare to sound their trumpets (vv. 2, 6). John saw seven angels who were given seven trumpets (v. 2) who prepared to sound their trumpets (v. 6). A warning is about to be given.

Another angel at the altar (vv. 3-5). In addition to the seven angels, John saw another angel standing at the altar[2] with a golden censer.[3] This angel was given much incense and mixed it with the prayers of the saints so those prayers ascended before God. The prayers of the saints are heard and answered.

Then the angel took the censer and filled it with fire from the altar and threw it to the earth causing noise, thunder, lightning, and an earthquake (v. 5). This symbolizes judgment upon the earth (i.e. upon Rome, the enemy of God's people). The prayers of the saints (vv. 3-4) prompted the judgment. Through their prayers, the Christians became victorious over Rome.

The scene of verses 1-6 sets the stage for the sounding of the seven trumpets.

Four Trumpets Sounded (vv. 7-12)

Trumpets were used throughout the Old Testament. They were used to call together a group (Num. 10:1-9). They were used to warn (Ezek. 33:3). Trumpets sounded an alarm (Hosea 5:8). In Joel, their use was for sounding an alarm and calling an assembly (2:1, 15). Here they are used to warn of coming judgment as a call to repentance.

The seven trumpets, like the seven seals and seven bowls of wrath (Rev. 15-16), "follow a uniform pattern with the first four being alike, followed by two, and then the final one."[4] Though commentators differ a little on the interpretation of each of the trumpets, it is agreed they are pointing to God's judgment upon Rome. Whatever these represent, it is the means by which God would bring Rome down. History will help us with our interpretation.

No interpretation is free of questions and problems, including the one presented in this work. "Any explanation of these phenomena which follow the trumpet sounds is generally unsatisfactory, even to the one who interprets. To interpret them literally and apply them to certain places and definite periods in history is impossible; to allegorize them leads into severe difficulties, although it is clearly evident that there was symbolical significance to the consequences which followed the trumpets. To view these evils as physical calamities which occurred throughout the Roman Empire is likewise not satisfactory. It can, however, be concluded with certainty that these trumpets represent warnings of a supernatural judgment from the Almighty."[5]

---

1 Ray Summers, *Worthy is the Lamb*, 154.
2 A reference to the altar of incense (Lev. 16:12-13).
3 "Usually a cup-shaped vessel on the end of a long handle (Lev 10:1) or a bowl sitting on a pedestal (Ezek 8:1). Censers were filled with incense and burning coals in order to emit a pleasant odor (Exod 25:38; 27:3; Lev 10:1; Ezek 8:11)" (Major Contributors and Editors. (2012, 2013, 2014, 2015). Censer. In J. D. Barry, D. Bomar, D. R. Brown, R. Klippenstein, D. Mangum, C. Sinclair Wolcott, ... W. Widder (Eds.), *The Lexham Bible Dictionary*).
4 Robert Harkrider, *Revelation*, 99.
5 Homer Hailey, *Revelation, An Introduction and Commentary*, 218-219.

First trumpet—Plant life burned up (v. 7). When the first angel sounded, hail and fire mixed with blood was thrown to the earth and burned a third of the trees and all the grass. One cannot help being reminded of the plagues upon Egypt. Here, when the first trumpet sounded, the plant life was burned up. There is little doubt that this refers to some natural calamity. The one third suggests that this is not a total, complete and final judgment.

Second trumpet—Sea creatures and ships destroyed (vv. 8-9). The second angel sounded and something like a great mountain burning with fire was thrown into the sea with a third of the sea becoming blood. A third of the sea creatures died as well as a third of the ships were destroyed. With the sea and sea creatures being affected, this too must refer to some form of natural calamity. The ships being destroyed may point to economic and commercial failure. Perhaps the latter is a result of a series of natural disasters.

Third trumpet—Waters became wormwood (vv. 10-11). With the third trumpet blast, a great star fell from heaven and fell on a third of the rivers and spring waters. The star's name was "Wormwood." A third of the waters became wormwood causing many to die from the bitter water.

This trumpet is a little more difficult. The rivers and spring waters being affected surely point to natural calamity.[6] Wormwood was a bitter plant used in the Old Testament in punishment of idolaters (Deut. 29:18; Jer. 9:15; 23:15). The point is that Rome will be made to drink (figuratively) waters poisoned with wormwood because of their rebellion against God. They will experience bitter suffering. We can't help but wonder if the star falling refers to the downfall of the one(s) in leadership.[7] Perhaps, as with the second trumpet, this comes as a result of a series of natural disasters.

Fourth trumpet—Sun, moon, and stars darkened (v. 12). The fourth angel sounded and a third of the sun, moon and stars were darkened. A third of the day and a third of the night had no light.[8] We are reminded that Egypt was burdened with darkness in the ninth plague (Exo. 10:21-29). This is not to be taken as some literal time when the sun, moon and stars will not shine. The judgment that God brings forth will be as if there was no light for a while. This trumpet seems to fit with the first three. Thus, it likely refers to some natural calamity.[9]

Similar language is used in the Old Testament to describe the overthrow or upheaval of a nation (Isa. 13:10), punishment of Egypt and its leader (Ezek. 32:7), judgment on Judah (Joel 2:10), judgment on the nations (Joel 3:15), God's dealing with evil in Israel (Amos 8:9), and the rulers and false prophets in Judah (Micah 3:6). Perhaps the downfall of the leaders is included as a result of natural calamity.

Summers recaps the four trumpets saying, "All these are pictures of natural calamity as an agent of destruction against Rome, the enemy of the Christian people. One of the main things that led to the breaking down of the Roman Empire was a series of natural calamities causing disaster over the empire: earthquake, volcanic eruption, floods, etc."[10]

---

6 Don't forget that the groups of seven (seals, trumpets and bowls) seemed to be grouped in a manner where the first four go together.
7 Similar language is used in the downfall of the king of Babylon (Isa. 14:12).
8 NKJV footnote.
9 Summers argues for natural calamity while Hailey and others make it more general.
10 *ibid.*, 156.

Harkrider summarized the trumpets thus, "Historians agree that the three major factors contributed to Rome's demise: natural calamity, internal rottenness, and outside invasion. It seems these three areas are symbolized, first, in the warning sounds of the trumpets, and again, but more completely, in the outpouring of God's wrath from the seven bowls which are yet to be revealed. The first four trumpets were pictures of natural calamity used by God as an agent of destruction. The fifth and sixth trumpets emphasize mankind's role in the downfall of Rome, and empire weakened by internal wickedness and finally overcome by external invasion. In this pageantry the symbolic details are used to make an impression. The lesson is missed if one attempts to interpret a meaning for each specific part of the vision rather than visualizing the scene in its entirety portraying a single message."[11]

Eagle Flying Announces Woes from Remaining Trumpets (v. 13)

Immediately John's attention is drawn to an eagle flying in the midst of heaven.[12] "The eagle is a symbol of vengeance in Deut. 28:49; Hos. 8:1; Hab. 1:8."[13] Thus, here it serves to warn of disaster that is coming. The eagle pronounces a triple woe (for emphasis of severity) concerning the three remaining trumpets. The warning is that more, and the worst, is yet to come.

Questions

1. What is the significance of silence in heaven for one half hour? _____
   _____

2. What is the point to be learned from the angel with the golden censer? _____
   _____

3. How do the prayers of the saints relate to the judgment upon Rome? _____
   _____

4. How are trumpets used throughout the Old Testament? _____
   _____
   _____

5. What happens when the first trumpet sounded and what does it mean? _____
   _____
   _____

6. What happens when the second trumpet sounded and what does it mean? _____
   _____
   _____

7. What happens when the third trumpet sounded and what does it mean? _____
   _____
   _____

---

11 Robert Harkrider, *Revelation*, 103.
12 The KJV and NKJV use the word "angel" in verse 13. The ASV and ESV and the footnote in the NKJV translate it "eagle."
13 M. R. Vincent, *Word Studies in the New Testament*, 2:507. See also Matthew 24:28.

8. What happens when the fourth trumpet sounded and what does it mean? _____
   _____
   _____

9. Historically what brings down Rome? _____
   _____
   _____

10. What does the eagle announce? _____
    _____
    _____

Revelation 9

Lesson 14
Fifth and Sixth Trumpets

Outline

I. **The Fifth Trumpet: The Locusts (vv. 1-12)**

   A. *Their source (vv. 1-3a)*
      1. Bottomless pit (vv. 1-2)
      2. Came upon the earth (v. 3a)

   B. *Their mission (vv. 3b-6)*
      1. Not to harm grass, any green thing or trees (v. 4)
      2. Not to kill those without the seal (v. 5)
      3. To torment those without the seal of God (vv. 5-6)
         a. Five months (v. 5)
         b. Victims seek death – cannot find it (v. 6)

   C. *Their description (vv. 7-10)*
      1. Shape – like horses prepared for battle (v. 7)
      2. Crown of gold (v. 7)
      3. Face like a man (v. 7)
      4. Hair like a woman's (v. 8)
      5. Teeth like a lion (v. 8)
      6. Breastplate like iron (v. 9)
      7. Sound of wings like chariots and many horses (v. 9)
      8. Tails like scorpions – sting (v. 10)

   D. *Their king (vv. 11-12)*

II. **The Sixth Trumpet: Angels and Horsemen (vv. 13-21)**

   A. *Four angels – to kill a third of mankind (vv. 13-15)*

   B. *Their army – the horsemen kill a third of mankind (vv. 16-19)*

   C. *Rest of mankind that were not killed – did not repent (vv. 20-21)*

Key Verses that Summarize the Chapter

Revelation 9:4, 15

⁴ They were commanded not to harm the grass of the earth, or any green thing, or any tree, but only those men who do not have the seal of God on their foreheads.

¹⁵ So the four angels, who had been prepared for the hour and day and month and year, were released to kill a third of mankind.

In the previous chapter, we saw the first four of the seven trumpets. Those four go together. We noted in the previous lesson that there seems to be a pattern of four being alike, followed by two, and then the final one. Those four dealt with one of the three major causes of the downfall of Rome—natural calamity. We have already suggested in lesson 13 that the fifth and sixth trumpets deal with the other two causes of the decline of Rome: internal rottenness and external invasion.

We must be careful to not miss the point while looking at the details of the imagery. "One is not to become so interested in the details of appearance that he misses the actor's 'lines.'"[1]

The Fifth Trumpet: The Locusts (vv. 1-12)

When the fifth trumpet sounded the locusts came upon the earth with a mission to torment those who did not have the seal of God. Some try to tie the locusts of the fifth trumpet with the horsemen of the sixth trumpet, making them the same. However, the eagle's announcement (8:13) indicates that they are distinct.

Their source (vv. 1-3a). John saw a star fall from heaven to the earth. This must have reference to Satan for the following reasons. He holds the key to the bottomless pit. He is later called Abaddon (Destruction) and Apollyon (Destroyer) in verse 11. Though the Bible never specifically tells us, the only reasonable explanation of the origin of Satan is that he is a fallen angel[2] (cf. 2 Pet. 2:4; Jude 6).[3]

The fallen star opened the bottomless pit[4] and so much smoke came forth that the sun and the sky turned dark (v. 2). Light is always associated with righteousness while darkness is associated with sin and evil. The fact that the smoke darkened the sky shows how much smoke and thus how much evil is involved.

Out of the smoke locusts came upon the earth. Locusts were a common pest in the Mid-East (Deut. 28:38; Joel 2:1-11, 25; 2 Chron. 7:13; Psa. 105:34; Nah. 3:15). The point to be learned here is that the source of the locusts is the bottomless pit. They came from Satan himself.

Their mission (vv. 3b-6). The locusts were given power to harm as scorpions have such power (v. 3b). They were not allowed to harm the grass, any green thing or the trees (v. 4). They were only to harm those who did not have the seal of God on their foreheads (v. 4). Those that are sealed (Rev. 7) are the faithful people of God. The locusts were not given authority to kill those without the seal, but could torment them for five months (v. 5). The five months is not to be taken as literal, but represents a definite or limited time. It is not seven months or ten months which might suggest something full or complete. God's punishment upon Rome is not complete with this woe.

The locusts (corruption and moral rottenness) would be so bad that men would rather die than live in the mess, but not be able to escape (v. 6).

---

1 Ray Summers, *Worthy is the Lamb*, 158.
2 Some have argued from Isaiah 14:12 thinking that "Lucifer" who was said to have "fallen from heaven" is a reference to Satan's origin. However, the context shows this is a reference to the king of Babylon (v. 4).
3 To argue otherwise would suggest that God created Satan.
4 See Revelation 11:7; 17:8; 20:1-3.

Their description (vv. 7-10). The vivid description of the locusts is probably given as much for the imagery as it is to indicate some quality about the corruption of society. However, some of the descriptions suggest the obvious. The appearance like horses (v. 7) points to their strength. The crown of gold (v. 7) may suggest their victory or success. The face of a man (v. 7) could tell us that their mission is accomplished in humans (the sin of the citizens of the nation). Having hair like a woman's (v. 8) may picture how appealing sin is.[5] Their devastating and devouring ability is seen in their teeth like a lion (v. 8). Their power is seen in the breastplate like iron (v. 9), the sound like chariots with many horses (v. 9), and in their tails that sting (v. 10).

Their king (vv. 11-12). Their king or ruler is none other than Satan himself. In Hebrew his name is Abaddom (meaning: Destruction) and in Greek it is Apollyon (meaning: Destroyer).

The fifth trumpet points to the internal rottenness that contributed to the destruction of Rome. "The best interpretation in the light of historical background seems to be that of Hengstenberg and Dana. They view this vision as symbolizing the hellish spirit which penetrates the earth (Hengstenberg) or the forces of decay which God has in his hand for retribution upon defiant Rome (Dana). It symbolizes the hellish rottenness, the internal decadence in the Roman Empire. One thing which brought about Rome's downfall was a series of corrupt rulers and leaders. Such a spirit of internal rottenness is pictured here as coming from within the empire (out of the earth) to work toward her destruction."[6]

Indeed, "Righteousness exalts a nation, but sin is a reproach to any people" (Prov. 14:34).

The Sixth Trumpet: Angels and Horsemen (vv. 13-21)

When the sixth angel sounded the second woe is revealed (cf. 8:13).

Four angels—to kill a third of mankind (vv. 13-15). John heard a voice from the four horns of the golden altar telling the sixth angel to release the four angels bound at the great Euphrates River. In the Old Testament the Euphrates was the place "where the great world powers of Old Testament times: Assyria, Babylon, Persia, arose and spread their devastating dominion over the world (16:12). ... 'At the river, the great one, Euphrates' does not place us at a geographical river or place but at the fountain of world dominance."[7]

These four angels were released to kill a third of mankind. As in the first trumpet, the one third suggests that this is not a total, complete and final judgment.

Their army—the horsemen kill a third of mankind (vv. 16-19). The number of the horsemen was two hundred million.[8] That is not a literal number, but simply portrays a great powerful number. The heads of the horses were like lions. Out of their mouths came three plagues (fire, smoke, and brimstone) by which they killed a third of mankind. In addition to the

---

5 Hailey references Vine as suggesting that the woman's hair points to their subjection to their Satanic master (cf. 1 Cor. 11:10, RV) (Homer Hailey, *Revelation, An Introduction and Commentary*, 230.
6 Summers, *ibid.*, 158.
7 R. C. H. Lenski, *The Interpretation of St. John's Revelation*, 302.
8 "In regular formation this would make a troop of cavalry one mile wide and eighty-five miles long!" Summers, *ibid.*, 158-159.

power of destruction in their mouths, their tails were like serpents with heads. All of this point to the fierce destruction of external forces.

Rest of mankind that were not killed—did not repent (vv. 20-21). "The rest of mankind" (those that are not in the third that were killed) did not repent of their evil deeds. The judgment that God brought upon Rome was designed to produce repentance. But, they did not change.

Note what we learn about repentance from this text. It involves the cessation of sin. They did not repent of the worship of demons and idols, etc. Thus, if they repented, they would not continue their evil deeds.

The sixth trumpet points to the external invasion that contributed to the destruction of Rome. "The whole picture presents the Parthian cavalry from the land of the Euphrates. This group was Rome's most dreaded enemy and a constant threat to her eastern boundary…. This whole picture is given to symbolize external invasion which would serve as an instrument in God's hand to punish the oppressors of his people."[9]

God used external forces to punish or destroy various nations. In the eighth century B.C., God used Assyria against Israel and Judah (Isa. 10:6-ff). In the seventh century B.C., God used the Chaldeans to destroy Assyria (Hab. 1:6-11). The Medes and Persians were used to conquer Babylon (Isa. 44:27 – 45:7; Jer. 51:11, 28).[10]

"The vision is given as a means of reassurance to the Christians to help them see that Rome will never triumph over Christianity."[11]

In these six trumpets we have seen the three major tools God used to bring down Rome: (1) Natural calamity (first four trumpets), (2) internal rottenness (fifth trumpet), and (3) external invasion (sixth trumpet).

Questions

1. What three major tools or means were used by God to bring Rome down? _____
_____
_____

2. What was involved in the fifth trumpet? _____
_____
_____

3. How were the locusts described? _____
_____

4. What did the fifth trumpet mean? _____
_____

---

9 Summers, *ibid.*, 159.
10 These examples are a summary of those given by Hailey, *ibid.*, 240.
11 Summers, *ibid.*, 160.

5. To what or whom did the star falling from heaven (v. 1) refer? _____
   _____

6. For class discussion: How did internal rottenness (a nation given to sin and corruption) destroy a nation or bring it down? _____
   _____
   _____

7. What was involved in the sixth trumpet? _____
   _____

8. What did the sixth trumpet mean? _____
   _____

9. What was the significance of a reference to the Euphrates? _____
   _____
   _____

10. Who were the rest of mankind (v. 20)? _____
    _____
    _____

Revelation 10 — Lesson 15
An Interlude: The Angel and the Little Book

Outline

I. The Angel and the Seven Thunders (vv. 1-7)

   A. *Description of the Angel (vv. 1-3)*
     1. Mighty (v. 1)
     2. Came down from heaven – clothed with a cloud (v. 1)
     3. Rainbow on his head (v. 1)
     4. Face like sun (v. 1)
     5. Feet like pillars of fire (v. 1)
     6. Book open in his hand (v. 2)
     7. Set one foot on sea and one on land (v.2)
     8. Cried with a loud voice (v. 3)

   B. *Sounding of seven thunders (v. 4)*

   C. *Angel's oath (vv. 5-7)*

II. John Eats the Little Book (vv. 8-11)

   A. *Voice from heaven said take the book (v. 8)*

   B. *John took the book and ate it (vv. 9-10)*

   C. *Angel said: "You must prophecy again…" (v. 11)*

Key Verses that Summarize the Chapter

Revelation 10:9

So I went to the angel and said to him, "Give me the little book." And he said to me, "Take and eat it; and it will make your stomach bitter, but it will be as sweet as honey in your mouth."

Here we have another interlude, placed between the sixth and seventh trumpet, just as one was placed between the sixth and seventh seal (chapter 7). This, the longest of the interludes, consists of two visions that present two pictures each. The first vision includes the angel and the seven thunders (10:1-7) and John eating the little book (10:8-11). The second vision involves the measuring of the temple (11:1-2) and the two witnesses (11:3-13). The point to be seen in this interlude is a message of swift divine retribution – the delay is over.

The Angel and the Seven Thunders (vv. 1-7)

Description of the Angel (vv. 1-3). The mighty angel came from heaven clothed in a cloud which indicates a divine mission—divine judgment. The rainbow about his head reminds us that God keeps his promises. Thus, the mission and message this angel brings are assurances that God is keeping his promises to his people. His face was like the sun and his feet was like pillars of fire (v. 1). Both point to divine authority and a divine mission.

The angel had a little book opened in his hand. The contents of the book will be discussed later in our comments at verse 8. Standing with one foot on the sea and one on the land may imply that his message is for the whole world, harmonizing with verse 11.

The angel cried out with a loud voice, as when a lion roars, so all could hear (v. 3). When he did, seven thunders sounded off. Thunder is used in connection with divine judgment and God's vengeance on evil (1 Sam. 2:10; 2 Sam. 22:14; Isa. 29:6).[1] This is more evidence of a divine mission and message.

Sounding of seven thunders (v. 4). We have seen seven seals, seven trumpets, and now seven thunders. Later, we will see seven bowls of wrath (Rev. 15-16). The seven thunders uttered their voices. Seven, being the complete number, tells us God's wrath and warning are full and complete (cf. v. 6).

John started to write due to the commission given earlier in the book (1:11, 19). However, he was told to seal them up and not write them. The warning of the six trumpets was sufficient to produce repentance. There would be delay no longer (cf. v. 6). There will be no more warning. So if it can't be told, why mention it at all? It serves to comfort the Christians and warn the enemy by demonstrating that there is even more than you see. There is even more than has been revealed.

Angel's oath (vv. 5-7). The angel raised his hand to heaven and swore by God (who lives forever and created all things) saying that there should be delay no longer (v. 6).[2] The point is that God's patience has ended. The day of pleas and warnings is over. The message (the delay is over – the mystery is finished) fulfilled what the prophets had said. God said he would establish a kingdom (in the days of the Roman empire) that would never be destroyed (Dan. 2:40-45). Domitian and his empire were trying to destroy the kingdom. Thus, when God vindicates his people and brings Rome down, that is just what the prophet said. Furthermore, Daniel 7:15-28 foretells of the kingdom of God being oppressed by the fourth kingdom (Rome), but would not prevail.

John Eats the Little Book (vv. 8-11)

Voice from heaven said take the book (v. 8). John was instructed to take the little book from the hand of the angel. What is the message of the little book? Some think it is the vision of chapter 11. Others think it is the message of the second section of the book (chapters 12-22). Yet others think it is a commission to preach God's judgment on the wicked.

---

1   Thunder is used throughout the book of Revelation (8:5; 10:3; 11:19; 16:18).
2   "There will be no more waiting" (NCV).

Ezekiel was told to eat a little book (Ezek. 2:8 – 3:3). His book was a message of sorrow and woe for a rebellious nation (Ezek. 2:7-8). This little book in Revelation has to allude to Ezekiel's little book. Thus, this too is a message of sorrow and woe for many - including Rome, any who rebel (the Christian who compromises), and the Christian who has to suffer for his faithful stand. The last verse of the chapter (v. 11) would seem to help us view this as a broad message for all people, nations and tongues.

John took the book and ate it (vv. 9-10). John was told to eat the little book. He was warned that it would make his stomach bitter, but be sweet as honey to the taste. Ezekiel's book was sweet to the taste (3:3), but indeed was bitter (3:14). The message was sweet for it was a message from God (cf. Psa. 19:10). It reveals the promises of God (the vindication of God's people). At the same time, it is bitter for it contains warnings and woes. The very deliverance of the message can be bitter.

So John took the little book and ate it (v. 10). He mastered its message and consumed it.

Angel said: "You must prophecy again..." (v. 11). Having consumed the message of the little book, John was told to prophecy about many peoples, nations, tongues and kings. God's message of woe is to be delivered to all.

So what is the point of this short chapter? It is a message of swift retribution. The delay is over. The message of woe is sent forth.

Questions

1. Describe the appearance of the angel that John saw. _____
   _____
   _____

2. What might the rainbow about the angel's head suggest? _____
   _____

3. What is to be learned from the angel having one foot on the sea and one on the land?
   _____
   _____

4. What is the significance of seven thunders? _____
   _____

5. Why was John told not to write what he heard in the seven thunders? _____
   _____

6. Why would the text mention the sounding of the seven thunders, but John be told not to write them? _____
   _____

7. What was the angel's oath? _____
   _____

8. What is the message of the little book that John ate? _____
_____

9. How could the book be bitter and sweet at the same time? _____
_____

10. What is the point of this interlude? _____
_____
_____

Revelation 11
Lesson 16
Measuring the Temple, Two Witnesses, and the Seventh Trumpet

Outline

I. **Measuring the Temple (vv. 1-2)**

   A. *John was told to measure the temple, altar and those who worship (v. 1)*

   B. *John was told to leave off the outside court (v. 2)*

II. **Two Witnesses (vv. 3-14)**

   A. *They would prophecy (vv. 3-6)*

   B. *They would be killed (vv. 7-10)*

   C. *They would be resurrected (vv. 11-14)*

III. **The Seventh Trumpet (vv. 15-19)**

   A. *Voice from heaven (v. 15)*

   B. *Twenty-four elders worship God (vv. 16-18)*

   C. *Temple of God opened in heaven (v. 19)*

Key Verse that Summarizes the Chapter

Revelation 11:15

Then the seventh angel sounded: And there were loud voices in heaven, saying, "The kingdoms of this world have become the kingdoms of our Lord and of His Christ, and He shall reign forever and ever!"

The first fourteen verses of this chapter are a continuation of the interlude that started at the beginning of the previous chapter. The first vision includes the angel and the seven thunders (10:1-7), and John eating the little book (10:8-11). The second vision involves the measuring of the temple (11:1-2) and the two witnesses (11:3-13). Both visions (involving the four pictures) deal with swift retribution – the delay is over. Here in the second vision, the point is to assure the people of God of victory. This is parallel in thought to chapter seven (the sealing of God's people).

Then, the last section of the chapter is the sounding of the seventh trumpet (vv. 15-19).

Measuring the Temple (vv. 1-2)

John was told to measure the temple, altar and those who worship (v. 1). In this vision, John was given a measuring rod and instructed by the angel to measure the temple, the altar and those who worship there. This was a vision and not to be taken as a reference to the literal temple.[1] Some have argued that this means the temple was still standing, and thus contend for an earlier date to the book.[2] The Premillennialist take this to imply that the temple will be rebuilt at the coming of Christ. Neither of these positions have any basis.

The temple symbolically refers to the church since it is called the temple of God (1 Cor. 3:16; Eph. 2:20-21). The measuring of the temple reminds us of Ezekiel, in a vision, measuring the temple and outer court (Ezek. 40-42) and Zechariah's vision of measuring Jerusalem (Zech. 2:2-5). In the case with Ezekiel, measuring the temple gave a picture of hope for the future. God will take care of his people. The measuring separated the holy from the common (Ezek. 42:20; 44:23). With Zechariah, the measuring was for protection and safety (Zech. 2:5). Hailey concludes, "The 144,000 who had been numbered and sealed unto God (7:1-4) are now represented as a 'measured temple' of worshipers, separated from the world and under divine protection."[3]

John was told to leave off the outside court (v. 2). John was instructed to leave off the outside court of the Gentiles. Those who were not the faithful of God would not be measured for separation and divine protection. That included the enemy—Rome.

The holy city will be trampled underfoot for forty-two months. The holy city must refer to the church (the people of God), because in this context it is the people of God who are being trampled by Rome. Forty-two months is three and a half years (half of seven) which is an incomplete or indefinite period.[4] "It symbolized uncertainty, restlessness, turmoil which had its turning point to the good or to the bad. So here it symbolizes God's protection over his own during an indefinite time of turmoil and difficulty while people generally are in the hands of godless Rome; however, this is not always to be. There is a turning point. God will see to that."[5]

Two Witnesses (vv. 3-14)

Who are the two witnesses that are introduced to us in verse 3? Many commentators have suggested two specific people (i.e. Moses and Elijah). Others have suggested that it is the Old and New Testaments. Neither of those explanations seems to make sense in the context.

The number two stands for power or strength. Two witnesses are required to establish one's word as true (Deut. 17:6; 19:15; 1 Tim. 5:19). The two witnesses in our text refer to the church (God's people) who would carry forth the gospel in the midst of the conflict with Rome. God calls them "my two witnesses" (v. 3). Thus, they are spokesmen for God. They

---

1   The fact that John is on the island of Patmos and a literal temple (if still standing) would be in Jerusalem makes a literal measurement of a literal temple impossible.
2   They conclude that it is before A.D. 70 (when Jerusalem and the temple were destroyed by the Romans).
3   Homer Hailey, *Revelation, An Introduction and Commentary*, 249.
4   Compare this to the time, times and half a time (Dan.7:25). Also forty-two months is the same as the 1260 days (Rev. 11:3; 12:6).
5   Ray Summers, *Worthy is the Lamb*, 163.

are enemies of the beast (v. 7). They are a torment to those who are wicked (v. 10). Thus, we conclude that these are not a literal number of two, but a reference to God's people preaching his word. This harmonizes with the point of the interlude—God assuring his people.

The text reveals three things about these two witnesses:

They would prophesy (vv. 3-6). They would prophesy one thousand two hundred and sixty days. That is the same period as forty-two months or three and a half years in verse 2. While they prophesy, they are clothed in sackcloth because of the oppression they face. The two witnesses are called two olive trees and two lampstands before God (v. 4). This probably refers to the light of the gospel they preach which comes from God. The two olive trees may suggest an endless supply of oil – meaning that the light will never burn out.

They would preach the gospel with success (v. 5). The fire proceeding out of their mouth devouring their enemies seems to symbolize that nothing could stop their success. Verse 6 may refer to the miracles that the apostles were able to perform.

They would be killed (vv. 7-10). The beast rising up, making war and killing them refers to the persecution that was designed to curtail the effectiveness of the two witnesses. Rome here is being used as a tool of Satan to fight against God. Their death will last for three and a half days (v. 9). Again, we have half of seven – an indefinite period that will come to an end.

They would be resurrected (vv. 11-14). After three and a half days the two witnesses (or prophets v. 10) come back to life.[6] A voice from heaven called them to "come up here" (v. 12). Their enemies witnessed their ascending to heaven. They triumph and overcome. The point here is to assure the people of God that they will be protected and vindicated.

"Thus ends the interlude, a message of divine retribution. There is to be delay no longer. God's message of judgment is to be proclaimed in all its bitterness. God's people are known and protected by him. There will be a strong witness of the gospel during this period of distress just ahead. When it is all over, Christianity will have been thoroughly vindicated in the sight of men."[7]

The interlude is over. The second woe is past (v. 14; 8:13). The third woe is coming (the seventh trumpet).

The Seventh Trumpet (vv. 15-19)

Voice from heaven (v. 15). When the seventh angel sounded, a voice from heaven said, "The kingdoms of this world have become the kingdoms of our Lord and of His Christ, and He shall reign forever and ever!" Here is a picture of victory through Christ. "This is a song of victory and rejoicing."[8] There is ultimate defeat and triumph as Christ conquers the world.

Twenty-four elders worship God (vv. 16-18). The twenty-four elders worshiped and praised God for the victory that was proclaimed by the voice in heaven. Note three elements in their praise:

---

6   We can't help but be reminded of the scene of Ezekiel 37.
7   Summers, *ibid.*, 166.
8   Summers, *ibid.*, 166.

1. God is in control (v. 17). He is the almighty. He is the one who was, who is and who is to come. With His great power, He reigns. God is still on this throne and in control (cf. Rev. 4).

2. The time for God's wrath has come (v. 18). The nations rage against God (cf. Psa. 2), and thus his wrath is stirred. The time has come that he should judge and destroy those who destroy the earth.

3. God will reward his people (v. 18). While the nations are judged and destroyed, God will vindicate and reward his saints.

The praise of the twenty-four elders is a summary of the message of the seven trumpets – God is in control, bringing the enemy of his people down, and victory to his people.

Temple of God opened in heaven (v. 19). The chapter closes with a scene of the temple of God open in heaven allowing the ark of the covenant to be seen. Then John saw and heard lightning, noise, thunder, an earthquake, and great hail. This is a reminder that God has not forgotten his covenant with his people. "These thunders, etc., are the symbols of omnipotent power in action."[9] God remembers his covenant and has the power and control to fulfill it.

So, what is the point of this chapter? The point is: there is victory for God's people and judgment by God on the enemy. John is encouraging his reader by saying that we may be down, but not out. We may lose a battle, but not the war.

Questions

1. What are the four pictures (given in two visions) in this interlude? _____

2. How could you respond to those who contend that verses 1-2 imply that the literal temple was still standing as John wrote? _____

3. What is the point of measuring the temple? _____

4. What is to be learned from leaving off the outside court of the Gentiles? _____

5. What is meant by the holy city being trampled for forty-two months? _____

6. Who are the two witnesses? _____

---

9 R.C.H. Lenski, *The Interpretation of St. John's Revelation*, 359.

7. What is the point to be learned from the two witnesses prophesying? _____
_____
_____

8. What is the point to be learned from the two witnesses being killed and resurrected?
_____
_____
_____

9. List the three points made in the praise the twenty-four elders offered. _____
_____
_____
_____
_____

10. What is the message to be gained from John seeing the temple opened and thus seeing the ark of the covenant? _____
_____
_____

Revelation 12

Lesson 17
The Woman and the Dragon at War

Outline

I. The Woman, The Dragon, and the Male Child (vv. 1-6)

   A. *The woman (vv. 1-2)*
      1. Clothed with sun (v. 1)
      2. Moon under her feet (v. 1)
      3. Garland of twelve stars on her head (v. 1)
      4. With child - cried out in labor pains (v. 2)

   B. *The Dragon (vv. 3-4)*
      1. Great fiery red dragon (v. 3)
      2. Seven heads (v. 3)
      3. Ten horns (v. 3)
      4. Seven diadems on head (v. 3)
      5. Tail drew third of stars and threw them to earth (v. 4)
      6. Stood before the woman to devour her child (v. 4)

   C. *The male child (vv. 5-6)*
      1. To rule nations with rod of iron (v. 5)
      2. Caught up to God on his throne (v. 5)
      3. Woman fled to wilderness for 1260 days (v. 6)

II. War In Heaven (vv. 7-12)

   A. *Michael and his angels fought against the dragon and his angels (v. 7)*

   B. *Great Dragon and his angels were cast out of heaven (vv. 8-9)*

   C. *Voice from heaven (vv. 10-12).*
      1. Now salvation, strength, kingdom and power have come (v. 10)
      2. Accusers have been cast down (v. 10)
      3. Our brethren overcame him (v. 11)
      4. Devil has come down to earth (v. 12)

III. Persecution of the Woman (vv. 13-17)

   A. *The dragon persecuted the woman (v. 13)*

   B. *The woman fled to the wilderness (v. 14)*

   C. *Serpent spewed water after the woman (vv. 15-16)*

   D. *Dragon makes war with the woman's offspring (v. 17)*

> **Key Verse that Summarizes the Chapter**
> **Revelation 12:17**
>
> And the dragon was enraged with the woman, and he went to make war with the rest of her offspring, who keep the commandments of God and have the testimony of Jesus Christ.

With this chapter we begin the second major section of the book.[1] The first section (1-11) focuses on the struggle on earth. This section (12-22) turns our attention to Christ and the Dragon in conflict – the deeper spiritual meaning. We are now going to see in this portion of the book what causes or drives the events of the first eleven chapters. The reason there is a conflict on earth between Rome and God's people is that there is a battle between Christ and Satan.

Chapters 1-11 picture victory from the vantage point of the Christian on earth. Chapters 12-22 picture victory from the vantage point of God in heaven.

Chapter twelve presents to us the woman and the Dragon at war.

The Woman, The Dragon, and the Male Child (vv. 1-6)

There are several characters introduced to us that must be identified to have clarity of understanding of this text (the woman, the dragon, the male child, etc.).

The woman (vv. 1-2). There are various thoughts about who the woman is. Some identify her as Mary, some as the Jewish nation, and others as the church. The woman is not a literal woman (Mary) any more than the dragon is literal. From the woman comes the male child (an obvious reference to the Christ, v. 5). The church did not produce the Christ, but Christ created the church (Matt. 16:18). "The woman can best be thought of as the spiritual remnant of God's people who, in faithfulness, had kept covenant with Him."[2] As evidence, Hailey cites Micah 4:10–5:3 where the daughter of Zion (the remnant) would be as a woman in labor pains until she had brought forth the Ruler in Israel.

She is pictured as being clothed with the sun, having the moon under her feet, and a garland of twelve stars on her head. These "symbolize her exalted position in God's order of things."[3] The woman cries out in labor pains ready to give birth (v. 2).

The Dragon (vv. 3-4). The dragon is Satan, the Devil (v. 9). He is described as great (powerful) and fiery red (v. 3) which may point to the fact that he is a murderer, guilty of bloodshed (John 8:44). His seven heads could suggest the wisdom he uses to accomplish his mission. The ten horns tell of his power. Seven diadems (crowns, the headdress of a king) tell of his authority and control. With his tail he casts down a third of the stars of heaven. Obviously, this says he has tremendous power and control. His influence extends over rulers, nations and even some angels (2 Pet. 2:4; Jude 6).

---

1 Go back to lesson 1 and review the outline of the book of Revelation.
2 Homer Hailey, *Revelation, An Introduction and Commentary*, 268.
3 Robert Harkrider, *Revelation*, 133.

The dragon (Satan) stood before the woman ready to devour her Child (the Christ). The conflict that is going on between Rome and the people of God is driven by a bigger battle between Satan and Christ.

The male child (vv. 5-6). The male child that was born is the Christ for he was destined to rule the world (v. 5). He was taken up into heaven (v. 4), a reference to his ascension (Acts 1:9-10). When he ascended he received his kingdom and ruled on his throne (Dan. 7:13-14; Eph. 1:20-21).

The woman fled to the wilderness for 1260 days (v. 6). As noted above, the woman is the spiritual remnant of Israel that now is spiritual Israel (the people of God, cf. v. 17). Since the male child was taken into heaven, the dragon's hatred for him is focused on the woman, thus the persecution that we see in chapters 1-11. She fled to the wilderness and is fed by God. That simply describes God's watchful care and protection for his people. She flees for 1260 days (same as 42 months or 3 ½ years, cf. 11:2-3) during the period of persecution.

War in Heaven (vv. 7-12)

The scene shifts from earth to heaven. A war is taking place in heaven. This conflict is the cause of the persecution of the woman who had the man child.

Michael and his angels fought against the dragon and his angels (v. 7). Michael is an angel leading in the battle against the dragon (Satan) and his forces. "Michael (מִיכָאֵל) signifies, 'Who is like to God?' We may compare this with the cry of the worldly in ch. 13:4, 'Who is like unto the beast?' In Daniel, Michael is the prince who stands up for the people of Israel (Dan. 12:1; 10:13, 21). Michael, 'the archangel,' is alluded to in Jude 9 as the great opposer of Satan. St. John, perhaps borrowing the name from Daniel, puts forward Michael as the chief of those who remained faithful to the cause of God in the rebellion of Satan and his angels."[4] The point is Michael and the host of angels fought against Satan and his forces.

Great dragon and his angels were cast out of heaven (vv. 8-9). The dragon (Satan) and his angels did not prevail. This may have reference to the death and resurrection of Christ. When Christ was crucified, it looked like the Devil had the upper hand. Yet, through his resurrection Christ delivered to Satan a devastating blow (cf. Gen. 3:15). Satan did not prevail.

Satan was cast out of heaven. This is not to be taken literally. This is not a discussion of the origin of Satan. He was cast out because he failed in his efforts to destroy the Christ. Summers describes Satan's battle against the Christ in terms of three campaigns. He sought to destroy Christ on earth. Then the second campaign was in heaven. He failed in both. Now he turns to fight in the third campaign against the woman who had the man child.[5]

The dragon is identified as "the serpent of old" (Gen. 3:1-6; 2 Cor. 11:3), "devil" (slanderer), and "Satan" (adversary).

Voice from heaven (vv. 10-12). A voice from heaven proclaimed victory. Through the death and resurrection of Christ, salvation and the kingdom are made possible. Through the same, strength and power is declared. Furthermore, through the crushing blow to Satan (the resurrection) the kingdom prevails over the opposition for the accuser has been cast down.

---

4   H. D. M. Spence-Jones, (Ed.), *Pulpit Commentary Revelation*, 312.
5   Ray Summers, *Worthy is the Lamb*, 173.

The faithful overcame by three things (v. 11): 1. The blood of the lamb. 2. The word of their testimony. "...their testimony involved unashamed confession before all – especially Roman provincial officials – of their belief that Jesus Christ is the Son of God (Luke 9:36)."[6] 3. They did not love their lives to the death. That is, they didn't regard their lives even in the face of the threat of death (cf. Rev. 2:10).

Satan has been cast to the earth to do his work for a short time (v. 12).[7] Though Satan fails to destroy the Christ, he is still out to destroy the church on earth. So, he makes war against the people of God through his tool, which is Rome. He knows his time is short and thus he uses that time to put on the pressure.

Persecution of the Woman (vv. 13-17)

The dragon persecuted the woman (v. 13). "Since the man child is beyond Satan's power to attack, the dragon seeks to hurt the child by persecuting the woman who gave Him birth."[8] We have already identified the woman as the spiritual remnant of God's people. By this point she represents the church being persecuted at the hands of Rome.

The woman fled to the wilderness (v. 14). The woman was given wings of a great eagle so she could fly into the wilderness. The wilderness represents God's watchful care, protection, and vindication of his people. The terminology of the "wings of an eagle" was used in describing God's deliverance of Israel from Egypt (Exo. 19:4; Deut. 32:11). A similar expression was used in anticipation of the return from Babylon (Isa. 40:31).

God will care for the woman (his people) for a time, times, and half a time. This is the same as the 1260 days (11:3; 12:6) and the forty-two months (11:2; 13:5).[9] The three and a half years (half of seven) is an incomplete, indefinite period of time.

Serpent spewed water after the woman (vv. 15-16). The serpent spewing water like a flood is symbolic of Satan's attempt to destroy the church.[10] God protected her by allowing the earth to swallow up the flood so that the woman is not destroyed. "The earth came to the woman's rescue through diverting Rome's attention by political uprisings, local wars, and other conflicts among subordinate kingdoms of the empire."[11]

Dragon makes war with the woman's offspring (v. 17). The "rest of her offspring" is another description of the church, the faithful of God who faithfully keep the commands and hold to the testimony of Jesus.[12] The dragon is out to destroy her, but he will not prevail.

So what is the point of this chapter? It is all a battle with Satan. He fights against the Christ from his birth to his death and then beyond to the people of God.

---

6   Harkrider, *ibid.*, 141.
7   The short time seems to be parallel with the "little while longer" (Rev. 6:11) that the martyrs will suffer.
8   Hailey, *ibid.*, 278.
9   Compare Daniel 7:25.
10 Similar language is used with reference to the threat of Assyria (Isa. 8:5-8).
11 Harkrider, *ibid.*, 144.
12 Compare ESV.

Questions

1. What is the contrast between the first major section of the book (chapters 1-11) and the last major section (chapters 12-22)? _____
   _____

2. Who or what does the woman represent? _____
   _____

3. Who or what does the dragon represent? _____
   _____

4. Who or what does the male child represent? _____
   _____

5. What is the Dragon's goal or purpose as revealed in this chapter? _____
   _____

6. What does it mean by "the dragon was cast out of heaven?" _____
   _____
   _____

7. How do the faithful overcome (v. 11)? _____
   _____

8. What does "they did not love their lives to the death" mean (v. 11)? _____
   _____
   _____

9. What does "times, time and half a time" mean (v. 14)? _____
   _____
   _____

10. What is the point or thrust of this chapter? _____
    _____
    _____

Revelation 13

Lesson 18
The Two Beasts

Outline

I. **The Beast of the Sea (vv. 1-10)**

   A. *Description (vv. 1-3a)*

   B. *Followers (vv. 3b-4, 8)*

   C. *Mission (vv. 5-7)*

   D. *Destiny – defeated (vv. 9-10, 18)*

II. **The Beast of the Earth (vv. 11-18)**

   A. *Description (v. 11)*

   B. *Mission and work (vv. 12-18)*

Key Verse that Summarizes the Chapter

Revelation 13:18

Here is wisdom. Let him who has understanding calculate the number of the beast, for it is the number of a man: His number is 666.

This chapter, the previous one and the one that follows comprise a section we have labeled as war (12-14).[1] In chapter 12, we saw the woman and the dragon at war. There we learned that the conflict and struggle we saw in chapters 1-11 is a conflict between God and Satan. The devil has been out to destroy the Christ since his birth. Now, at the writing of this book, he is seeking to destroy the church.

In this chapter we see two beasts. Both are allies of Satan and antagonistic to the church. Understanding chapters 12-14 is a key to understanding the rest of the book.

The Beast of the Sea (vv. 1-10)

Who or what is the beast of the sea? Beasts were used by Daniel to symbolize the four great world empires and their rulers (Dan. 7:2-8). These four beast came up out of the sea (Dan.

---

[1] Go back to lesson one and look at the outline of the book.

7:2-3). The sea represents the mass of humanity or society. The sea is referenced several times in Revelation (8:8; 10:2,8; 12:12; 13:1; 20:13; 21:1). Daniel's fourth beast is the fourth kingdom of the world which is the Roman empire (Dan. 7:23).[2] The description, nature and work of this beast of the sea fit the Roman empire (or more particularly Domitian as the emperor). That understanding harmonizes with the context of the book. He is a tool of Satan, the dragon (v. 2). He accepts worship (v. 4). His power is only for limited time (v. 5). He is a powerful ruler (v. 7).

Description (vv. 1-3a). The beast John saw had seven heads (v. 1). This may refer to the wisdom with which he accomplishes his purpose or mission. Or it may refer to his durability (cf. v. 3). The ten horns (v. 1) may indicate the great power he has. The ten crowns on one of his horns (v. 1) may point to his authority and rule over many (cf. v. 7). The blasphemous name no doubt refers to the claim he made to be the Supreme Lord God and demanded others worship him by saying "Caesar is Lord."

The sea beast is compared to a leopard, a bear, and a lion (cf. Dan. 7). All of these tell us how fierce and vicious he is in carrying out the mission for Satan.

Commentators differ over the meaning of one of his heads being mortally wounded and yet was healed (v. 3a).[3] Some think that the beast (the empire) received a blow to one of his heads in the death of a previous emperor (i.e. Nero) who persecuted the people of God. His work and mission of persecution was revived in Domitian. "The death of Nero dealt a severe blow to the empire, which was immediately thrown into a two-year state of anarchy and confusion. Order was restored by Vespasian of the Flavian family. But to the church, which is John's interest, the healing of the death-stroke came with the revival of persecution under Domitian."[4]

Followers (vv. 3b-4, 8). All the world (v. 3b) and all who dwell on the earth (v. 8) would be the majority of people within the Roman empire. Those who follow him offer worship by burning incense and saying "Caesar is Lord!" Those who do so do not have their name in the Lamb's Book of Life (v. 8). Those that have their names in the book refuse to worship him. His worshippers proclaim his power by asking who can possibly make war with him (v. 4).

Mission (vv. 5-7). The beast spoke blasphemies against God, his name, his tabernacle and those who dwell in heaven (vv. 5-6). Domitian certainly blasphemed the name of God when he claimed to be the "Supreme Lord and God" and demanded the citizens of the empire to worship him saying he is "Lord." Daniel's vision of the four beasts pictured the ruler of the fourth kingdom (Rome) as speaking "pompus words against the Most High" (Dan. 7:25).

His work is limited to 42 months (v. 5). That is the period of 1260 days (12:6) and the 42 months or 3 ½ years that we have already seen (11:2-3; 12:14). It is an incomplete, indefinite period of time.

He is given authority (from the dragon, making him a tool of Satan) to make war (persecute) with the saints (v. 7). His authority as a world emperor is over every tribe, tongue and nation (v. 7).

---

2   The previous ones were Babylon, Medo-Persian, and Grecian empires as was seen in Daniel 2.
3   Homer Hailey cites Pieters as listing ten varying interpretations (*Revelation, An Introduction and Commentary*, 286).
4   Hailey, *ibid.*, 286.

Destiny —defeated (vv. 9-10, 18). The sea beast will be defeated. He who leads to captivity and kills (Domitian and his empire) will go into captivity and be killed (will be defeated). His number is 666 (v. 18). That number is explained later in this lesson. However, it points to his failure and defeat. Understanding this picture will develop the patience (endurance) and faith (stronger faith) of the saints (v. 10).[5]

The Beast of the Earth (vv. 11-18)

Who or what is the beast of the earth? Two things help identify this beast. First, he works under the authority of the first beast (v. 12). Second, his mission is to enforce the worship of the first beast (vv. 12, 15). This leads us to believe that this represents some arm of the Roman government that was used to see that the citizens of the empire conformed to emperor worship. "All these characteristics seem to identify the second beast as the 'Commune' or 'Concilia" set up in Asia Minor to enforce the state religion."[6]

Description (v. 11). The beast that arose out of the earth had two horns like a lamb and spoke like a dragon. The lamb may suggest the religious nature of the beast – enforcing the state religion. The two horns may point to limited power of this beast in contrast to the full power of the Lamb who had seven horns (cf. 5:6). The voice of the dragon shows that he speaks with the authority of Satan who is the dragon of the previous chapter.

Mission and work (vv. 12-18). As already noted above, this beast functions under the authority of the first beast, the Roman empire or emperor (v. 12). The mission is to cause all those who dwell in the earth to worship the first beast (v. 12). He performs "signs" and thus deceives many (vv. 13-14). Perhaps the power to work "signs" could be like that of Pharaoh's magicians who were allowed to work wonders, but did not measure up to God's signs (Exo. 7:10-12). Jesus warned that false prophets would arise, show great signs and wonders, and deceive many (Matt. 24:24). Paul warned that the work of Satan would involve signs and lying wonders (2 Thess. 2:9). The "signs" were a deception (v. 14).

The earth beast was given power to give life to the image of the first beast (v. 15). Pulpit Commentary observed, "he gives it an appearance of reality which a mere image could not possess."[7] Hailey suggests this means he makes Ceasar-worship live and speak the mind of the empire.[8] Summers proposes this arm of the Roman government was given power to build images of Domitian and altars at the images and legislate any way they could to enforce such worship.[9] By enforcing this worship, those who refused were threatened to be killed (v. 15).

---

5   The ESV renders this, "Here is a call for the endurance and faith of the saints."
6   Ray Summer, *Worthy is the Lamb*, 178.
7   H. D. M. Spence-Jones, (Ed.). *Pulpit Commentary, Revelation*, 335.
8   Hailey, *ibid.*, 295.
9   Summers, *ibid.*, 179.

Those who bowed and worshipped the emperor were marked on their right hand and foreheads (v. 16).[10] Only those who had that mark could buy and sell in the marketplace (v. 17). Thus, one of the forms of persecution was that Christians (who would not worship Caesar) were pressured by not being able to buy or sell. "Worshipping the emperor was a test at every phase of life. Christians were boycotted in the market for refusal to bear the mark of the emperor. Marriage settlements, wills, transfers of property – none of these were legal without the stamp of the emperor."[11]

The number of the beast (the sea beast) is 666. Efforts have been made to connect this number to the Pope, Napoleon, Nero, Martin Luther, and Hitler. None of those would have any meaning to the recipients of the book. The safest method is to interpret in light of the symbolism of the day. Six falls short of the perfect seven. Thus, it stands for evil or failure. "The number '6' awakened a feeling of dread in the breast of the Oriental who felt the significance of numbers. It fell short of the sacred '7' and was an evil number. To the Oriental there was doom in the number '6' when it stood alone. Raise it to a series – '666' – and there is a representation of the potency of evil than which there can be no greater, a direfulness of fate than which there can be no greater. By symbol the number '666' is evil raised to its highest power."[12] Hailey observes that the 6 being short of seven symbolizes that which is imperfect and destined to fail. Thus, tripled to 666 it represents complete and utter failure and doom.[13] Thus, his number means failure, failure, failure.

The basis of this chapter: Rome (its emperor and the Concilia) is a mere tool of Satan and is destined to fail.

Questions

1. Who or what is the beast of the sea (vv. 1-10)? _____

2. What evidence can be given for your answer to the previous question? _____

3. What is meant by the statement that "the beast was mortally wounded and then healed?" _____

4. How long does the sea beast operate and what does that mean? _____

5. Who or what is the beast of the earth (vv. 11-18)? _____

---

10 Some think this was a literal mark or brand. However, we have little or no information to confirm that. It very well may simply be a figurative expression to denote those who pledge allegiance to Domitian.
11 Summers, *ibid.*, 179.
12 Summers, *ibid.*, 177.
13 Hailey, *ibid.*, 299.

6. What evidence can be given for your answer to the previous question? _____
   _____

7. What is the role or mission of the beast of the earth? _____
   _____

8. What is one way the beast of the earth enforces emperor worship? _____
   _____

9. What does the number 666 mean? _____
   _____

10. Summarize this chapter. What is the main point? _____
    _____
    _____
    _____

Revelation 14

Lesson 19
The Victorious Lamb

Outline

I. **The Lamb and 144,000 on Mount Zion (vv. 1-5)**

   A. *Name of the Father on their foreheads (v. 1)*

   B. *Worshipped God with a new song (vv. 2-3)*

   C. *144,000 are followers of the Lamb (vv. 4-5)*

II. **Messages from Heaven (vv. 6-13)**

   A. *First angel: "Fear God and give glory..." (vv. 6-7)*

   B. *Second angel: "Babylon is fallen" (v. 8)*

   C. *Third angel: "If any worship the beast – tormented" (vv. 9-12)*

   D. *Voice from heaven: "Blessed are the dead..." (v. 13)*

III. **Harvest Time (vv. 14-20)**

   A. *Son of man reaps the earth (vv. 14-16)*

   B. *Angel gathers for the winepress of wrath (vv. 17-20)*

Key Verse that Summarizes the Chapter

Revelation 14:1

Then I looked, and behold, a Lamb standing on Mount Zion, and with Him one hundred and forty-four thousand, having His Father's name written on their foreheads.

This chapter concludes the section we have labeled as war (12-14).[1] In chapter 12 we saw the woman and the dragon at war. In chapter 13 we saw the emperor and the Roman Concilia as allies of Satan that will be defeated. This chapter pictures victory for the Lamb and his followers. When the saints who are suffering at the hands of Rome see this picture of victory, it should cause great joy and celebration.

---

1 Go back to lesson one and look at the outline of the book.

The Dragon (chapter 12) uses two instruments to accomplish his mission (seen in chapter 13). Likewise, God uses two instruments to gain victory: The Lamb and the sickle (judgment) revealed in this chapter. We will see three things in this chapter: the Lamb and 144,000 on Mount Zion (vv. 1-5), four messages from heaven (vv. 6-13), and a picture of harvest time (vv. 14-20).

The Lamb and 144,000 on Mount Zion (vv. 1-5)

John saw the Lamb (the Christ) standing on Mount Zion. Zion was first used to refer to the city of David—Jerusalem (2 Sam. 5:7; 1 Chron. 11:5). It was the city of the great king (Psa. 48:2). It was a place of refuge, safety and security (Psa. 48:3, 13; 20:2; 125:1; Isa. 14:32). The gospel was to go forth out of Zion, which is Jerusalem (Isa. 2:3; Micah 4:2).

Mount Zion is used in Hebrews 12:22-24 to refer to the heavenly Jerusalem—heaven. So, here in our text it seems to refer to the heavenly Jerusalem.[2] Here is a scene of victory of the Lord standing on Mount Zion. With him are the 144,000 (cf. chapter 7) who are the faithful of God.

The number, 144,000, is not a literal number just as in chapter 7. As it was used in chapter 7, the sea was not literal. The four corners of the earth were not literal. The twelve tribes were not literal. Here in this chapter if the 144,000 is literal, then so are the virgins (v. 4), and the men (those who were not defiled with women - v. 4). That would mean the 144,000 could not include women or anyone who is married.[3] If this is a literal number, then there could not be 144,001.

This number suggests the idea of completeness. It is a multiple of 12 (the religious number) multiplied by 1000. Not one of the faithful will be lost.

Name of the Father on their foreheads (v. 1). In contrast to those who worship the beast who had the mark of the beast on their forehead (13:16), the 144,000 have their Father's name on their forehead as a mark of identity (cf. 7:3).

Worshipped God with a new song (vv. 2-3). John heard a voice like the voice of many waters and like a loud thunder. He also heard harpists playing their harps. Then he heard the 144,000 singing a new song (cf. 5:9). This, no doubt, was a song of victory and celebration for it could only be known and sung by the 144,000.

144,000 are followers of the Lamb (vv. 4-5). The 144,000 had not defiled themselves with women (v. 4). That is, they had not committed spiritual fornication by worshipping the beast of the sea (Domitian). They were virgins – spiritually pure (v. 4). They follow the Lamb wherever he goes (v. 4). They were completely dedicated and loyal in the service of Christ. In their mouth is found no deceit (v. 5). They had not denied the Christ or proclaimed that Caesar is Lord. They stand, without fault, before the throne of God.

---

2 Hailey takes the view that it is not describing a heavenly scene but the "Zion of the Messiah" to which the saints have come (*Revelation, An Introduction and Commentary*, 302).
3 See Wayne Jackson, *Revelation: Jesus Christ's Final Message of Hope*, 57.

Messages from Heaven (vv. 6-13)

Here we see four messages from heaven. The first three are attributed to angels. The last is from a voice in heaven. All four messages announce the triumph of the Lamb and his people over the evil that is set against them.

First angel: "Fear God and give glory..." (vv. 6-7). The first angel has the everlasting gospel that is to be preached to all men (cf. Matt. 28:18-19; Mark 16:15-16) and cries with a loud voice, "Fear God and give glory to Him, for the hour of His judgment has come" (v. 7). Rather than fearing Domitian and his forces, and giving him praise and honor, one should fear God and give glory to him. The reason given is that the hour of judgment has come. This is not the final judgment in the end of time, but judgment upon Rome. "All this indicates that the victory of the Lamb is so certain that an angel messenger announces the triumph and victory before the battle is fought."[4]

The everlasting gospel is the message of salvation in Christ that is to be preached to the world (Mark 16:15-16).[5] As victory over Rome has come, the preaching of the gospel flourishes again. The message of the first angel ends with a call to worship Him who is the creator of the world (v. 7b).

Second angel: "Babylon is fallen" (v. 8). The second angel said, "Babylon is fallen, is fallen..." This is the first mention of Babylon in the book of Revelation (16:19; 17:5; 18:2, 10, 21). This statement alludes to Isaiah 21:9 or Jeremiah 51:8 where judgment was pronounced against Babylon. Here in our text, Babylon is Rome, the oppressor of God's people as Babylon of old was. The assurance that Babylon will fall is so great that it is spoken in past tense as if it is already accomplished.

The reason given is that "she has made all nations drink of the wine of the wrath of her fornication." That is because she has made others commit spiritual fornication by bowing in worship to the emperor. This seems to be taken from Jeremiah 51:7. Babylon of old made all nations drink of her wine. Hailey quotes Alford saying, "'Two things are mingled: (1) the wine of her fornication, of which all the nations have drunk (17:2); and (2) the wine of the wrath of God which He shall give her to drink, v. 10 and 16:19. The latter is retribution for the former: the former turns into the latter: They are treated as one and the same.' (Alford, p. 688)."[6]

Third angel: "If any worship the beast – tormented" (vv. 9-12). The third angel announced doom upon those who worship the beast and his image. Those who do will drink the wine of God's wrath in full strength (cf. Psa. 75:8; Jer. 25:15-38). This alludes to the practice of mixing water with wine to dilute it. But here, God's wrath will be in its full strength. They will be tormented with fire and brimstone (a reference to eternal damnation). The smoke of their torment ascends forever and ever (v. 11).[7]

---

4   Ray Summers, *Worthy is the Lamb*, 181.
5   Summers takes the "gospel" to refer to good tiding of God's victory (*ibid.*, 181).
6   Hailey, *ibid.*, 308.
7   This passage refutes the doctrine of annihilation. Those who are punished in hell don't cease to exist forever and ever, but are tormented forever and ever. Compare this with Revelation 4:9 where we see God lives "forever and ever." That means an endless future. Thus, the torment is an endless future.

Knowing this calls for patience (endurance, perseverance) of the people of God (v. 12).[8]

Voice from heaven: "Blessed are the dead..." (v. 13). The fourth message was attributed to a voice from heaven who commanded John to write this message. In contrast to those who die outside of the Lord (vv. 10-11), those who die in the Lord (including those who die as martyrs for the cause of the Lord) will be blessed. They will rest from their labors (hard work under the pressure of persecution). Their works follow them (they will be rewarded according to their faithfulness).

Harvest Time (vv. 14-20)

The final section of the chapter is a harvest scene—a picture of divine judgment. Students differ over whether this is a reference to a judgment in time or the final judgment. Also, there is a question of whether this is a picture of judgment in general or a picture of judgment (vindication) on the righteous (vv. 14-16) and on the wicked – Rome (vv. 17-20). In this context, it seems more reasonable to conclude that this is a judgment in time and not the final judgment.

There seems to be a difference in verses 14-16 and verses 17-20. That leads us to think that the righteous are under consideration in the first instance and the wicked Rome in the later.[9]

Son of man reaps the earth (vv. 14-16). John looked and saw a white cloud[10] which may suggest purity or holiness. On the cloud sat one like the Son of Man which is an obvious reference to Christ (cf. Dan 7:13). The golden crown on his head says he is the king who rules and conquers. The sickle in his hand depicts him as executing judgment.

An angel came out of the temple (speaking for God) and told the Son of Man to reap the harvest of the earth for it was ripe. We do not take this to be the final judgment, but a vindication of the righteous. "This first harvest (grain) seems to refer to gathering righteous ones (Matt. 3:12; 9:37-38; John 4:35-38). For them the struggle is over, and the cause for which they suffered will now be vindicated. This harvest is distinguished from the one to follow in which the wicked ones, represented by the cluster of grapes, are cast into the winepress of God, as announced by the fifth and sixth angels."[11]

Angel gathers for the winepress of wrath (vv. 17-20). Two more angels come into the scene. The first comes out of the temple (a messenger of God) with a sharp sickle. The second angel comes out from the altar and has power over fire. This may refer to the angel that took the golden censer, filled it with fire from the altar and cast it to the earth (8:3-5). This angel tells the one with the sickle to thrust it to the earth and gather grapes for the great winepress of the wrath of God. The winepress is used of divine judgment (Joel 3:13; Isa. 63:1-6; Lam. 1:15). This harvest scene is a picture of judgement on Rome. The grapes are fully ripe (v. 18) which says the time has come because their sin is full and complete.

---

8   The ESV renders this, "Here is a call for the endurance of the saints." The NIV translates it, "This calls for patient endurance on the part of the people of God who keep his commands and remain faithful to Jesus."
9   Summers concludes this is not a distinction in the righteous and wicked, but a general picture of judgment against evil (*ibid.,* 183).
10 Clouds were used to symbolize judgment upon Egypt and Jerusalem (Isa. 19:1; Jer. 4:13; Matt. 24:30; 26:64).
11 Robert Harkrider, *Revelation,* 169-170.

The vision John sees has blood coming out of the winepress up to the horses' bridles for 1200 furlongs (200 miles). Obviously this is not literal, but merely shows the severity and magnitude of the judgment against Rome.

So what is the point of this chapter? It is a picture of victory and judgment. With this chapter we conclude the section labeled in our outline as "War." Chapter 12 made the point that it is all a battle with Satan. Chapter 13 made the point that Rome (which is an ally or tool of Satan) will fail. Chapter 14 is a picture of victory for God and his people.

"The forces of evil are strong: the devil and his two allies, Antichrist and Roman Concilia. But the forces of righteousness are stronger: God with his two allies, the Victorious Christ and Divine Judgment. As the curtains close on this scene, there is rejoicing in the hearts of those who watch the pageant."[12]

Questions

1. How do we know the 144,000 is not literal? _____

2. If the 144,000 is not literal, then to whom or what does the number refer? _____

3. Give a summary of the first section of this chapter (vv. 1-5). _____

4. Give a summary of the second section of this chapter (vv. 6-13). _____

5. Give a summary of the third section of this chapter (vv. 14-20). _____

6. What is the message of the first angel (vv. 6-7)? _____

7. What is the message of the second angel (v. 8)? _____

8. What is the message of the third angel (vv. 9-12)? _____

---

[12] Summers, *ibid.*, 183.

9. What is the message of the voice from heaven (v. 13)? _____
_____
_____

10. Is there a contrast or difference in verses 14-16 and 17-20? If so, what is it? _____
_____
_____
_____

Revelation 15 & 16

Lesson 20
Seven Bowls of Wrath

Outline

Revelation 15
Seven Angels with Seven Bowls of Wrath

I. Seven Angels with Seven Plagues of Wrath (v. 1)

II. The Victorious Saints on the Sea of Glass (vv. 2-4)

    A. *Those that overcame (v. 2a)*
       1. The beast
       2. The image of the beast
       3. The mark and number of the beast

    B. *Singing the song of Moses and the Lamb (vv. 2b-4)*

III. Seven Bowls of Wrath Given to the Seven Angels (vv. 5-8)

    A. *Seven angels come out of the temple (vv. 5-6)*

    B. *One of the four living creatures gave seven bowls of wrath to the seven angels (v. 7)*

    C. *Temple filled with smoke of the glory of God (v. 8)*

Key Verse that Summarizes the Chapter

Revelation 15:1

Then I saw another sign in heaven, great and marvelous: seven angels having the seven last plagues, for in them the wrath of God is complete.

Both chapters 15-16 deal with the seven bowls of wrath and are grouped together. Chapter 15 introduces us to the seven angels who are given the seven bowls of wrath. Chapter 16 lists the seven bowls that are poured out on the earth.

We read of a contrast between the victory of the saints (standing on the sea of glass) in chapter 15 with the judgment executed upon the wicked in the seven bowls of chapter 16. This same contrast is seen throughout the book. Chapter 7 is a picture of victory in the sealing of the 144,000 in contrast to the sounding of the seven trumpets in chapters 8-9. In chapter 14, we see the victorious lamb in contrast to the four voices announcing judgment at the end of the chapter.

The seven seals reveal God's judgment. The seven trumpets warn of God's judgment. The seven bowls of wrath execute God's judgment.

Chapter 15 serves as an introduction to chapter 16.

Seven Angels with Seven Plagues of Wrath (v. 1)

You now recognize the number seven represents completeness. Here we consider seven angels with seven last plagues (bowls of wrath). In these plagues the wrath of God is complete. Up to this point, the picture has been partial (incomplete) judgment. The seals were on a fourth of the earth (6:8). The trumpets were upon a third (8:10, 11, 12; 9:15, 18). The time has come to execute God's complete judgment upon Rome.

The Victorious Saints on the Sea of Glass (vv. 2-4)

Before we see the bowls of wrath, we are treated to a victorious picture of God's saints. The victorious saints are standing on a sea of glass. We were introduced to the sea of glass before the throne (4:6) which told us that the throne of the exalted God is unapproachable, at least for the present.[1] Later we see a time when there is no more sea (Rev. 21:1). Here in the present chapter, is a picture of the saints (already dead) who did not compromise, standing on that sea that approaches the throne of God. The sea was mingled with fire. The fire may be from their persecution. "This item not in 4:6 (a vision of peace), but here it adds to the splendour of the vision. This parenthesis (2 to 4) gives a picture of the martyrs in their state of bliss."[2]

Those that overcame (v. 2a). Those standing on the sea had victory over the beast, the image of the beast and the number of his name. Though martyrs, they overcame the beast because they did not compromise or bow to pressure.

Singing the song of Moses and the Lamb (vv. 2b-4). These victorious saints are celebrating their victory by singing the song of Moses and the Lamb. The song of Moses was a song of deliverance from the land of Egypt (Exo. 15). In this song (recorded in verses 3-4), God is praised for his power and might which brings victory.

Seven Bowls of Wrath Given to the Seven Angels (vv. 5-8)

Seven angels come out of the temple (vv. 5-6). John saw the "temple of the tabernacle of the testimony in heaven" opened. This is not the literal temple of Solomon's day or even the temple built by Herod. John, in a vision, is allowed to see this temple of the tabernacle in heaven. The ESV renders this "the sanctuary of the tent of witnesses." As Barnes observes, this "does not refer to the whole of the building called the 'temple,' but to the holy of holies."[3] Thus, this likely refers to the inner sanctuary of the tabernacle. It is called the tabernacle of witness because it was a witness or testimony of the presence of God among his people

---

1 John was able to approach it only in a vision.
2 A. T. Robertson, *Word Pictures in the New Testament* (Rev. 15:2).
3 Albert Barnes, *Notes on the New Testament: Revelation*, 355.

(cf. Num. 9:15; 17:7; Acts 7:44). No doubt this scene is to remind the people of God that he has not forgotten his people.

The angels' appearance in bright linen and golden bands, coming out of the tabernacle, suggests they are on a divine mission.

One of the four living creatures gave seven bowls of wrath to the seven angels (v. 7). One of the four living creatures[4] around the throne of God gave the seven angels bowls of wrath to be poured out on the earth. This wrath (judgment) was coming from God who lives forever and ever – in contrast to Rome and its emperor, neither of which lasts for long.

Temple filled with smoke of the glory of God (v. 8). Smoke filled the tabernacle (Exo. 40:34-ff) and the temple (1 Kings 8:10-ff) at the dedication of each. In this vision, John sees the temple (tabernacle) filled with the smoke of God's glory and power. The smoke remained and no one could enter until the seven plagues (seven bowls) were completed.

There is no time or place for intercession. The day of repentance is gone. It is time to execute the wrath of God.

The point of this chapter is the victory of God's people in contrast to the judgment to be poured out in the next chapter.

Outline

Revelation 16
Seven Bowls of Wrath

I. **First Bowl: on the Earth (v. 2)**

   A. *Causes a foul and loathsome sore*

   B. *Upon those who have the mark of the beast and worship his image*

II. **Second Bowl: on the Sea (v. 3)**

   A. *Sea became blood*

   B. *Creatures of the sea died*

III. **Third Bowl: on the River and Springs (vv. 4-7)**

   A. *Water turned to blood (v. 4)*

   B. *Angels praised God for righteous judgment (vv. 5-7)*
      1. Angel of the waters
      2. Angel from the altar

---

[4] See Revelation 4:6, 8; 5:6, 8, 14; 6:1, 6; 7:11; 14:3; 19:4.

IV. Fourth Bowl: on the Sun (vv. 8-9)

A. *Scorched men with fire (v. 8)*

B. *Men who were scorched (v. 9)*
   1. Blasphemed God
   2. Did not repent
   3. Did not give glory to God

V. Fifth Bowl: on the Throne of the Beast (vv. 10-11)

A. *Kingdom of the beast becomes full of darkness (v. 10a)*

B. *Beast and his kingdom (vv. 10b-11)*
   1. In pain
   2. Blasphemed God
   3. Did not repent

VI. Sixth Bowl: on the Euphrates (vv. 12-16)

A. *River dried up – making way for kings of the earth (v. 12)*

B. *Three unclean spirits go out to gather kings to battle (vv. 13-16)*
   1. From the Dragon, beast and false prophet (v. 13)
   2. Go to kings to gather them for battle (v. 14)
   3. A warning (v. 15)
   4. At Armageddon (v. 16)

VII. Seventh Bowl: into the Air (vv. 17-21)

A. *Voice from the temple of heaven: "it is done" (v. 17)*

B. *Noises, thunder, lightning and earthquake (v. 18)*

C. *Effect of this fierce wrath (vv. 19-21)*
   1. Cities of nations fall
   2. Wrath poured upon Babylon
   3. Men blasphemed God

Key Verse that Summarizes the Chapter

Revelation 16:1

Then I heard a loud voice from the temple saying to the seven angels, "Go and pour out the bowls of the wrath of God on the earth."

The seven angels were instructed by a loud voice to go pour out the bowls of wrath on the earth (v. 1). The time has come for judgment to begin. This is judgment in time and not a reference to the final judgment in the end of time. The number seven tells us this judgment is complete.

The identity of each bowl proves to be difficult. However, we are certain about two things: (1) The seven bowls are God's judgment upon Rome that will bring it down. (2) The means by which Rome falls include natural disaster, internal rottenness, and external invasion. These are included in the seven bowls, yet we are hard pressed to be dogmatic about how those fit into this chapter. Summers observed, "No attempt to determine the special meaning of the objects thus visited by the wrath of God – land, sea, rivers, sun – has yet been or is ever likely to be successful. The general effect of God's final retributive wrath alone appears to be important."[5] While this is true, we will make some suggestions about possibilities, though we cannot be dogmatic about them.

The seven bowls are very similar to the plagues upon Egypt (Exo. 7-12).

First Bowl: on the Earth (v. 2)

Causes a foul and loathsome sore. The first angel poured his bowl upon the earth which caused a foul[6] and loathsome[7] sore upon men (cf. Exo. 9:10). Corruption is breaking out among men. This may refer to the internal rottenness of sin and evil from within that contributed to the downfall of Rome.

Upon those who have the mark of the beast and worship his image. Those upon whom the sores appeared were given to the worship and service of the beast (the Roman emperor).

Second Bowl: on the Sea (v. 3)

Sea became blood. The second angel poured his bowl on the sea and it became blood as of a dead man. The sea often represented society or the mass of humanity (cf. Rev. 13:1; Dan. 7:2-8, 17, 23). Thus, this possibly refers to a society given over to sin – dead in sin.

Creatures of the sea died. Perhaps this is a picture of the permeating nature of consequences of sin. "A society abandoned to idolatry and its consequent morals, as was the Roman Empire of John's day, is spiritually dead. In such a society, morals decline to the lowest level; the family collapses, schools breed anarchy and rebellion, business ethics are forgotten, entertainment becomes base and sordid, and printing presses exude smut and filth, until the whole is strangled in its own death blood and suffocated by its own stench. Our society too must listen to the trumpet warnings before God pours out the bowls of wrath."[8]

---

5   Ray Summers, *Worthy is the Lamb*, 186.
6   NKJV footnote, "lit. *bad and evil.*"
7   The word translated "loathsome" in this verse "emphasizes the activity of evil" (M. R. Vincent, *Word studies in the New Testament*, 2:539).
8   Homer Hailey, *Revelation, An Introduction and Commentary*, 328.

Third Bowl: on the River and Springs (vv. 4-7)

Water turned to blood (v. 4). The third angel poured his bowl on the rivers and springs, and they became blood. The significance of this is revealed in the angels' reaction (vv. 5-7).

Angels praise God for righteous judgment (vv. 5-7). The angel of the waters praised God for being righteous in his judgment (v. 5). God gave those, who shed the blood of the saints, blood to drink which was their "just due" (v. 6). An angel from the altar praised God for his righteous judgments (v. 7). Thus, the third bowl is about divine retribution – divine justice upon Rome.

Fourth Bowl: on the Sun (vv. 8-9)

Scorched men with fire (v. 8). The fourth angel poured his bowl out on the sun and was given power to scorch men with fire. Verse 9 points to judgment upon the evil men. Perhaps this includes the leadership in the Roman empire as well as those who pledged loyalty through emperor worship.

Men who were scorched (v. 9). Those who were punished blasphemed God, refused to repent and give glory to the one true God. Rather than responding to God's judgment by changing, they added to their sins.

Fifth Bowl: on the Throne of the Beast (vv. 10-11)

Kingdom of the beast becomes full of darkness (v. 10a). The fifth angel poured out his bowl on the throne of the beast (identified in chapter 13 as the Roman emperor). This points to the fall of the emperor, who at the moment seems to be so powerful that he cannot fall. His kingdom, however, will be full of darkness.

Beast and his kingdom (vv. 10b-11). Because of the judgment in this bowl, the beast and his kingdom are in pain, they blasphemed God and refused to repent.

Sixth Bowl: on the Euphrates (vv. 12-16)

River dried up—making way for kings of the earth (v. 12). When the sixth angel poured out his bowl on the Euphrates river, its waters dried up making way for the kings from the east to enter. In the Old Testament, the enemies of God's people (Assyria and Babylon) were east of the Euphrates River. The prophets of old used the river to refer to their enemies (Isa. 7:20; 8:7; Jer. 46:10). The Parthians (who invaded Rome) were to the east of the river as well. This sixth bowl no doubt refers to the external invasion.

Three unclean spirits go out to gather kings to battle (vv. 13-16). Three unclean spirits, like frogs, come out of the dragon's mouth (the devil), the mouth of the beast (the Roman emperor – Domitian), and the mouth of the false prophet (the second beast of chapter 13 – the Roman Concilia). These evil or unclean spirits, functioning like generals preparing for a battle, go out to the kings of the earth and gather them for help in the battle (v. 14). To gain followers, deception is used (v. 14).

The Lord warns his people to watch and keep their garments for he is coming as a thief (v. 15). This is not a reference to the final judgment, but a judgment in time upon Rome.

The battle took place at Armageddon[9] (v.16). Armageddon literally means mountain of Megiddo. "The word is compounded of the Hebrew *Har* mountain, and *Megiddon* or *Megiddo: the mountain of Megiddo*."[10] Megiddo was located in the valley of Jezreel (West Manasseh). It was the site of many decisive battles (Jud. 5:19; 2 Kings 9:27; 23:29; 2 Chron. 35:20-25). Thus, Armageddon simply stands for a decisive battle between the forces of Satan and the Lamb of God. More details about the battle is given in Revelation 19:19-21. The battle is not a literal battle any more than literal frogs are generals leading in the battle.[11]

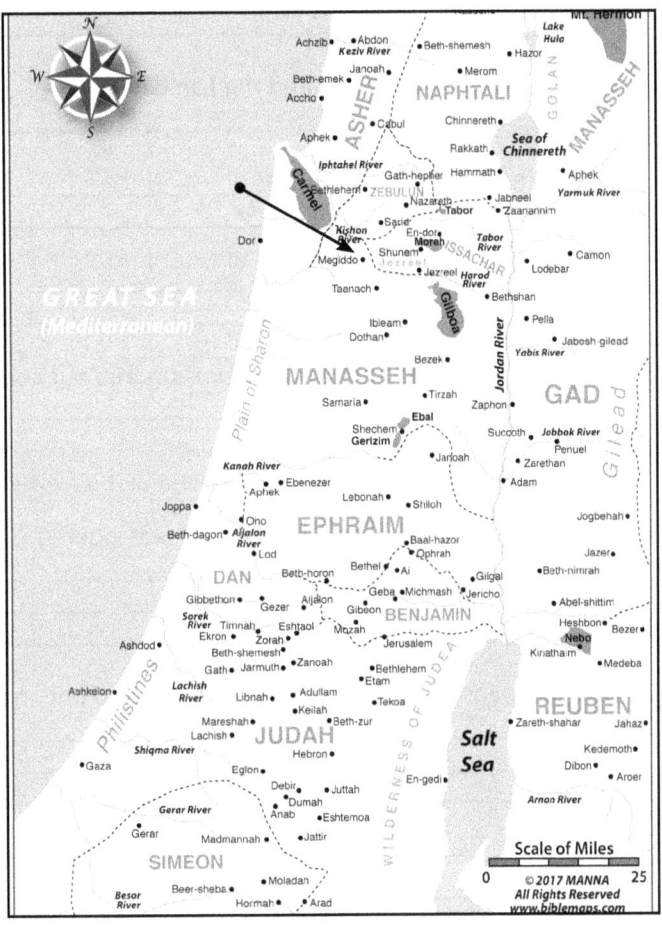

Seventh Bowl: into the Air (vv. 17-21)

Voice from the temple of heaven: "it is done" (v. 17). When the seventh angel poured out his bowl into the air, a voice from the throne of heaven said, "It is done." The point: judgment is complete.

Noises, thunder, lightning and earthquake (v. 18). The noises, thunderings, lightnings and an earthquake are symbols of judgment. The earthquake was greater than any earthquake since men were on the earth. This symbolizes the power of God in executing his wrath on Rome.

Effect of this fierce wrath (vv. 19-21). The great city (Rome) was divided into three parts.[12] The nations fell. Here is a picture of the total collapse of the empire. The cup of wrath is so severe that there is no place for refuge (vv. 20-21).

The time has come for God's wrath to be executed upon Rome according to Chapter 16.

---

9 ASV: Har-Magedon.
10 M. R. Vincent, *Word Studies in the New Testament*, 2:542.
11 The premillennialists abuse this verse claiming it is a literal war to be fought just before the earthly reign of Christ on earth. They ignore the symbolic nature of the book. This battle has already been fought for the events in the book were to shortly take place (1:1, 3; 22:6, 10).
12 Compare this with Ezekiel 5:2 where Jerusalem was divided into thirds.

Questions

1. Who is standing on a sea of glass in chapter 15? _____
   _____

2. What is the song of Moses and the Lamb? _____
   _____

3. What is the point of chapter 15? _____
   _____

4. What is the point of chapter 16? _____
   _____

5. What happens when the first bowl was poured out and to what does it possibly point?
   _____
   _____

6. What happens when the second bowl was poured out and to what does it possibly point? _____
   _____
   _____

7. What happens when the third bowl was poured out and to what does it possibly point?
   _____
   _____
   _____

8. What happens when the fourth bowl was poured out and to what does it possibly point?
   _____
   _____
   _____

9. What happens when the fifth bowl was poured out and to what does it possibly point?
   _____
   _____
   _____

10. What happens when the sixth bowl was poured out and to what does it possibly point?
    _____
    _____
    _____

11. What happens when the seventh bowl was poured out and to what does it possibly point? _____
    _____
    _____

Revelation 17

Lesson 21
The Great Harlot

Outline

I. John's Vision of the Great Harlot (vv. 1-6)

   A. *One of the seven angels shows John the judgment of the great harlot (v. 1a)*

   B. *Description of the great harlot (vv. 1b-6)*
   1. Sits on many waters (v. 1b)
   2. Committed fornication with kings and inhabitants of the earth (v. 2)
   3. Sitting on a scarlet beast (v. 3)
      a. Full of names of blasphemy
      b. Sevens heads
      c. Ten horns
   4. Appearance (v. 4)
   5. Golden cup full of abomination and fornication in her hand (v. 4)
   6. Message on her forehead: "Mystery, Babylon the Great..." (v. 5)
   7. Drunk with blood of saints and martyrs (v. 6)

II. Explanation of the Mystery (vv. 7-18)

   A. *The Beast (vv. 8-14, 16-17)*
   1. Was, is not, and yet is (v. 8)
   2. Destined for destruction (vv. 8, 11)
   3. Seven heads (vv. 9-10)
      a. Seven mountains
      b. Seven kings
   4. Ten horns are ten kings (vv. 12-14, 16-17)
      a. a. Have no kingdom yet, but receive authority with the beast (vv. 12-14, 17)
      b. b. Make war with the lamb – lamb will be victorious (v. 14)
      c. c. They hate the harlot and devour her (v. 16)

   B. *The Harlot (vv. 15, 18)*
   1. Waters are the people and nations (v. 15)
   2. The woman is the great city (v. 18)

Key Verse that Summarizes the Chapter

Revelation 17:1

Then one of the seven angels who had the seven bowls came and talked with me, saying to me, "Come, I will show you the judgment of the great harlot who sits on many waters."

This chapter and the next are devoted to the fall of Babylon, the harlot.[1] Babylon is used here to refer to Rome (the great enemy of God's people as Babylon of old was a great enemy). It is called "Babylon the Great" (v. 5). Literal Babylon wouldn't fit into the context of the book, but Rome certainly would. It is called a great city (v. 18). Rome fits that as well. The seven mountains (v. 9) is "Referring, undoubtedly, to Rome—the seven-hilled city."[2] The wickedness of ancient Babylon is here attributed to Rome (cf. Rev. 14:8; 16:19). Language similar to what is found in our text was used in the Old Testament to describe the fall of Babylon (Jer. 51:7-13).

John's Vision of the Great Harlot (vv. 1-6)

One of the seven angels shows John the judgment of the great harlot (v. 1a). One of the seven angels that had poured out a bowl of wrath announced he would show John the judgment of the great harlot. Rome is called a harlot for she had seduced many to commit spiritual fornication by enforcing emperor worship (cf. v. 2).

Description of the great harlot (vv. 1b-6). John saw the harlot sitting on many waters (v. 1b). The waters represent people (v. 15) which alludes to the size and influence of the empire. She committed fornication with kings and inhabitants of the earth (v. 2) by causing them to worship the beast.

The scene changed and John saw the harlot sitting on a scarlet beast (v. 3). This no doubt is the same beast of chapter 13 (the Roman emperor). The harlot sitting on the beast points to how the emperor supports and carries the empire (cf. v. 7). The beast was full of names of blasphemy (he called himself the Supreme Lord God and demanded others worship him saying "Caesar is Lord"). The beast has seven heads (cf. 13:1) which are explained later in verse 9. He also has ten horns (cf. 13:1) which may indicate the great power he has.

Her appearance (v. 4), like any harlot, makes her attractive to seduce and entice the world to that which is evil. The golden cup (from which one would expect something pure) is full of abomination and fornication (v. 4). The message or name on her forehead, "MYSTERY, BABYLON THE GREAT, THE MOTHER OF HARLOTS AND THE ABOMINATIONS OF THE EARTH" (v. 5), identifies who she is and what she is. She causes many to wonder at her (vv. 6-7). She is the mother of harlots in that she is responsible for many becoming harlots through her evil influence.

She was drunk with the blood of saints and martyrs (v. 6). Rome was responsible for the death of the saints that did not bow to the pressures of emperor worship (cf. 6:9-11).

Explanation of the Mystery (vv. 7-18)

The angel, that had shown the harlot to John, said he would explain to him the woman and the beast that he had seen (v. 7).

The Beast (vv. 8-14, 16-17). The beast seen by John is the same as the beast of the sea in chapter 13, which we have identified as the Roman emperor. He is described as the one who "was, and is not, and yet is" (v. 8; cf. 13:3). This may refer to a lull in persecution after

---

1 Go back to lesson 1 and look at the outline of the book of Revelation.
2 Albert Barnes, *Notes on the New Testament: Revelation*, 386.

the death of Nero but was revived under the rule of Domitian. The beast is destined for perdition (destruction; vv. 8, 11) which is a reference to eternal destruction rather than the downfall of his empire.

The angel says to John, "Here is the mind which has wisdom" (v. 9). "These words (as in ch. 13:18) draw attention to the explanation which follows—or else that which precedes (cf. ch. 13:18). They also make it appear that the explanation which the angel offers of the 'mystery' is not one to be understood without some difficulty."[3] The seven heads are the seven mountains on which the harlot sits (v. 9) - a reference most likely to the seven hills on which Rome sits. However, rather than the literal hills, the seven mountains are the seven kings in verse 10.[4] These are not seven literal kings or emperors, for we would be hard pressed to know which ones to identify as the seven since there were more than that in the history of the empire. Any attempt to do so would be pure guesswork. The number seven is likely used to stand for the whole or complete group of kings or emperors. "The seven kings, therefore, were a symbolic number, representing all kings or kingdoms, past, present, and future that would oppose the kingdom of God. Each who would come would still be part of the seven."[5]

"Since seven represents the whole, five is a broken, incomplete number. This suggests that of the total number of kings who have been and shall be, the greater part have come and gone. One refers to the current reigning power. The seventh king is yet to reign, and that only for a brief time."[6]

The beast is said to be the eighth and yet of the seven (v. 11). How can that be? If the numbers are symbolic, then being the eighth may simply mean that in him was "so essentially combined and concentrated all that there was in the seven."[7] The point seems to be that Domitian and the Roman Empire were so corrupt that they were the embodiment of all the evil kingdoms represented.

The ten horns are ten kings (vv. 12-14, 16-17). Ten (not a literal number) suggests power. This most likely refers to kings of the provinces who serve under the rule of the beast (vv. 12-14, 17). They obey and submit to the emperor (v. 13). These make war with the Lamb for making war with the people of God is to make war with the Lamb (v. 14). The Lamb will be victorious (v. 14).[8]

Back to the ten kings, they will hate the harlot and devour her (v. 16). The provincial kings will turn on Rome and contribute to her destruction.

The Harlot (vv. 15, 18). The waters are the people and nations (v. 15) which describe her power and influence as an empire. The woman (the harlot) is the great city (v. 18) which is none other than Rome. In the next chapter, we see her fall announced.

---

3   H. D. M. Spence-Jones, *Pulpit Commentary Revelation*, 416.
4   The ASV renders verse 10, "and they are seven kings;..." The ESV renders the same verse, "they are also seven kings,..."
5   Homer Hailey, *Revelation, An Introduction and Commentary*, 353.
6   Robert Harkrider, *Revelation*, 198.
7   Albert Barnes, *Notes on the New Testament: Revelation*, 387.
8   Here is a summary verse of the book. The conflict on earth is a conflict with the forces of Satan and the Lamb of God. The Lamb will march away victorious.

"Such great importance was attached to Rome as the center of the persecuting power of the first century that three whole chapters are given to portray her doom."[9]

Questions

1. Why is Rome referred to as Babylon the great? _____
_____
_____

2. Who or what is the great harlot? _____
_____

3. Why is she called the mother of all harlots? _____
_____
_____

4. What does the harlot sitting on many waters represent? _____
_____
_____

5. What does the harlot sitting on a scarlet beast represent? _____
_____
_____

6. What is meant by the description "was, and is not, and yet is" (v. 8)? _____
_____
_____

7. Who are the seven kings of verse 10? _____
_____
_____

8. How can the beast be the eighth and yet of the seven (v. 11)? _____
_____
_____

9. Who are the ten kings (vv. 12-14, 16-17)? _____
_____
_____

10. What is meant by the ten kings will hate and devour her (v. 16)? _____
_____
_____

---

[9] Ray Summers, *Worthy is the Lamb*, 191

Revelation 18

Lesson 22
The Fall of Babylon the Harlot

Outline

I. **The Announcement from Heaven of Her Fall (vv. 1-8)**

   A. *Angel with great authority said (vv. 1-3)*
   1. Babylon is fallen, is fallen (v. 2a)
   2. Babylon has become (v. 2b)
      a. A habitation of demons
      b. A prison for every foul spirit
      c. A cage for every unclean and hated bird
   3. The reason for her fall (v. 3)
      d. Nations have drunk of the wine of the wrath of her fornication
      e. Kings have committed fornication with her
      f. Merchants became rich through her luxury

   B. *Another voice from heaven said (vv. 4-8)*
   1. "Come out" to God's people who dwell in her (v. 4)
   2. She will receive her just reward (vv. 5-8)

II. **Those Who Mourn Her Fall (vv. 9-19)**

   A. *Kings of the earth (vv. 9-10)*

   B. *Merchants (vv. 11-17a)*

   C. *Shipmasters (vv. 17b-19)*

III. **Her Fall Causes Rejoicing (v. 20)**

   A. *In heaven*

   B. *Among those avenged by her fall*

IV. **The Finality of Her Fall (vv. 21-24)**

   A. *Illustrated by the angel throwing a stone into the sea (v. 21)*
   1. Babylon will be thrown down
   2. Shall not be found anymore

   B. *All activity will cease in her (vv. 22-23)*
   1. Amusement life
   2. Business life
   3. Home life

   C. *Reason: she had slain prophets and saints (v. 24)*

> **Key Verse that Summarizes the Chapter**
> **Revelation 18:2**
>
> And he cried mightily with a loud voice, saying, "Babylon the great is fallen, is fallen, and has become a dwelling place of demons, a prison for every foul spirit, and a cage for every unclean and hated bird!

Chapters 17-18 form a unit of chapters devoted to the fall of Babylon, the harlot. The previous chapter identified the Roman empire as Babylon, the great harlot. This chapter announces her fall. The language used to describe her demise is very similar to the prophecy against Babylon of old (Isa. 13:19-22; 21:9; Jer. 50:39-40; 51:8).

The Announcement from Heaven of Her Fall (vv. 1-8)

Angel with great authority said (vv. 1-3). An angel with great authority stated three things about the fall of Babylon.

1. Babylon is fallen, is fallen (v. 2a). This is the main point being made by the angel (and the thrust of the chapter). Though yet in the future, it is described as in the past because of the assurance that it will happen. The words are taken from Isaiah 21:9 (cf. Rev. 14:8). The announcement of her fall serves to encourage the people of God who have suffered at her hand.

2. Babylon has become... (v. 2b). Babylon (Rome) has become so corrupt that it is a dwelling place for demons, a prison for foul spirits, and a cage for every unclean and hated bird. Similar language is used in Isaiah 34:11-15; Jeremiah 51:37; and Zephaniah 2:14. "The utter desolation of Babylon is vividly described when it is said that even the unclean spirits and the unclean and hated birds consider it a prison."[1]

3. The reason for her fall (v. 3). The nations have drunk of the wine of the wrath of her fornication (cf. Jer. 51:7; Rev. 14:8). The kings have committed fornication with her. Both expressions refer to how Rome had enforced the state religion (emperor worship) and thus caused many to commit spiritual fornication. The merchants have become rich through her luxury. The ESV renders it, "the merchants of the earth have grown rich from the power of her luxurious living." The nations have joined in adultery with her in an effort to benefit from her power and wealth.

Another voice from heaven said two things (vv. 4-8). First, John heard another voice from heaven saying to the people of God to come out of her lest they participate in her sins and receive the same due to her (v. 4).

Second, the voice said the harlot would receive her just reward (vv. 5-8). Her sins have reached the heavens (v. 5). She would receive judgment that is according to her evil deeds (vv. 6-7). In her pride she sees no danger of her fall (v. 7).[2] Thus, her plagues (judgment) are

---

1 William Hendriksen, *More Than Conquers*, 207.
2 Babylon had said the same things boasting she would never fall (Isa. 47:7-11).

coming in one day (v. 8; one hour, v. 10, 17, 19) which means it is coming quickly, suddenly and with certainty. Here is a picture of a sudden reversal: she quickly goes from queen to widowhood.

Those Who Mourn Her Fall (vv. 9-19)

There are three categories of people who weep for Rome. They mourn for the simple reason that her downfall is their own downfall. They go down with her.

Kings of the earth (vv. 9-10). The kings of the earth are those who had formed an alliance with Rome which involved them in the spiritual fornication with her (v. 9). They are utterly amazed at how quickly the mighty nation collapsed (v. 10). She doesn't have her power anymore.

Merchants (vv. 11-17a). "Rome was built upon two things: territorial conquest and trade expansion."[3] The merchants mourn for no one buys their merchandise anymore (v. 11). Their mourning over her is more about themselves and their loss – their economic ruin. All kinds of goods are listed in verses 12-14 that are no longer traded because of her fall. The bodies and souls of men (v. 13) may refer to slave trade. The merchants, like the kings, are shocked at how soon the mighty rich nation came to nothing (v. 17a).

Shipmasters (vv. 17b-19). The shipmasters who had become rich by trade with Rome weep and wail over their loss because of her fall. They, like the kings and merchants, are astonished at how soon she is laid waste (v. 19).[4]

Since those who became rich because of Rome go down with her, we must conclude as Summers did, "Nothing can be economically good if it is morally bad."[5]

Her Fall Causes Rejoicing (v. 20)

The only ones who are rejoicing are those in heaven, the apostles, prophets, and the faithful of God for they have been vindicated by her fall. The NCV renders this verse, "Be happy because of this, heaven! Be happy, God's holy people and apostles and prophets! God has punished her because of what she did to you."

The Finality of Her Fall (vv. 21-24)

The rest of the chapter is devoted to a picture of the finality of Rome's fall. Three things are stated in this section:

Illustrated by the angel throwing a stone into the sea (v. 21). The mighty angel took a great millstone[6] and threw it into the sea. Similar language was used of Babylon of old (Jer. 51:63-64). Just as the stone was thrown into the sea never to be recovered, so Babylon will be thrown down not to be revived again. "Those who oppose this method of interpretation

---

3   Ray Summers, *Worthy is the Lamb*, 194.
4   Footnote in NKJV.
5   *ibid.*, 194.
6   "The millstones were about 2 feet in diameter and ½ foot in thickness" (Albert Barnes, *Notes on the New Testament: Matthew & Mark*, 262).

point out the fact that Rome still stands. That is true, but it is not the persecuting Rome of John's day."[7]

All activity will cease in her (vv. 22-23). The hustle of a busy city will be no more. Three areas are identified: Amusement life[8] is affected. The sound of music will not be heard anymore. Business life is impacted as well. No craftsman will be found in the city. The sound of the millstone grinding will not be heard anymore. Home life is touched as well. The voice of the bridegroom and the bride will not be heard.

Reason: she had slain prophets and saints (v. 24). Babylon (Rome) will fall because she has slain (or at least allowed the slaying) of the prophets and saints.

So what is the point of this chapter? It is the fall of Rome. "All through this section the main thing in the writer's mind is the fall of Rome."[9]

We cannot read this chapter and not walk away with an impression of how sin destroys a nation. "Righteousness exalts a nation, but sin is a reproach to any people" (Prov. 14:34). William Barclay said, "This is the fate of a city that built a civilization without God."[10]

Questions

1. Why is the fall of Babylon (Rome) spoken of in past tense when its fall was yet future?
   _____
   _____

2. What reason(s) is given for the fall of Rome? _____
   _____

3. How does Rome view the possibility of her fall? _____
   _____

4. Who mourns for the fall of Babylon the Harlot? _____
   _____

5. Why do the kings mourn her fall? _____
   _____

6. Why do the merchants mourn her fall? _____
   _____

7. Who rejoices over her fall and why? _____
   _____

---

7   Summers, *ibid.*, 195.
8   These three expressions are taken from Summers, *ibid.*, 194-195.
9   Summers, *ibid.*, 193.
10 William Barclay, *Revelation*, 2:216.

8. What is the point to be made by the angel throwing the millstone into the sea? ____
   _____
   _____

9. What is the main point of this chapter? _____
   _____
   _____

10. If Rome is to be no more, how could that be since Rome still exists today? _____
    _____
    _____

Revelation 19
Lesson 23
Victory Over the Harlot and the Beast

Outline

I. **The Celebration in Heaven (vv. 1-10)**

    A. *Great multitude praises God saying (vv. 1-3)*
        1. "Alleluia! Salvation and glory and honor and power belong to the Lord our God!" (v. 1)
        2. "True and righteous are His judgments" (v. 2a)
        3. "He has judged the great harlot" (v. 2b-3)

    B. *Twenty-four elders and the four living creatures worship God (v. 4)*

    C. *Voice from the throne said, "praise our God..." (vv. 5-10)*
        1. Heard a multitude praising God (vv. 6-9)
        2. John rebuked for worshipping the angel – told to worship God (v. 10)

II. **Christ the Victorious Warrior (vv. 11-21)**

    A. *Christ on a white horse (vv. 11-16)*
        1. He is called (vv. 11, 13, 16)
            a. Faithful and True (v. 11)
            b. Word of God (v. 13)
            c. King of kings (v. 16)
            d. Lord of Lords (v. 16)
        2. Judges and makes war (vv. 11, 14-15)
        3. Description (vv. 12, 13, 15)
            a. Eyes like a flame of fire (v. 12)
            b. Many crowns (v. 12)
            c. Robe dipped in blood (v. 13)
            d. Sharp sword coming out of his mouth (v. 15)

    B. *The defeat of the beast and his armies (vv. 17-21)*
        1. Birds invited to eat carcasses of armies (vv. 17-18, 21)
        2. Beast captured and cast in lake of fire (vv. 19-20)
        3. Armies of the beast killed (v. 21)

> **Key Verses that Summarize the Chapter**
> **Revelation 19:2, 20**
>
> [2] For true and righteous are His judgments, because He has judged the great harlot who corrupted the earth with her fornication; and He has avenged on her the blood of His servants shed by her."
>
> [20] Then the beast was captured, and with him the false prophet who worked signs in his presence, by which he deceived those who received the mark of the beast and those who worshiped his image. These two were cast alive into the lake of fire burning with brimstone.

With this chapter we begin a section labeled in our outline of the book as "Victory of God's people" (19-21).[1] Having seen the fall of Babylon the harlot (17-18), the scene shifts to the celebration in heaven for the victory over the harlot and the beast (19). The next chapter deals with the victory over Satan (20), while the third focuses on the victory in heaven (21).

The Celebration in Heaven (vv. 1-10)

This chapter is the contrast to those who mourn the fall of the great harlot in the previous chapter (18). Here the celebration is not so much for her fall as it is the vindication and victory of the people of God.

Great multitude praises God saying (vv. 1-3). A new scene opens wherein John hears the voice of a great multitude (the triumphant saints) praising God for their victory. Three statements of praise offered by the multitude are recorded:

1. "Alleluia! Salvation and glory and honor and power belong to the Lord our God!" (v. 1). Alleluia (Hallelujah) means Praise the Lord.[2] God is praised for his glory, honor and power.

2. "True and righteous are His judgments" (v. 2a). God is praised for his just judgment (cf. 16:7).

3. "He has judged the great harlot" (v. 2b-3). God is praised for his judgment on the great harlot (chapter 18) because of her fornication, thus avenging the martyrs she had slain. Again, the multitude said, "Alleluia, Her smoke rises up forever and ever" (v. 3). "The destruction of Rome was not pictured as that of a city which burns to the ground and where men go in to remove the wreckage. It is pictured as an eternal destruction, an eternal burning."[3]

Twenty-four elders and the four living creatures worship God (v. 4). The twenty-four elders and the four living creatures (introduced to us in in the throne scene in chapter 4) praise God saying "Amen! Alleluia."

---

1 Look back to the outline of the book found in lesson 1.
2 This word is found in the New Testament only in this chapter (vv. 1, 3, 4, 6).
3 Ray Summers, *Worthy is the Lamb*, 196.

Voice from the throne said, "praise our God..." (vv. 5-10). Next, John hears a voice from the throne calling for those who fear God to give praise to God (v. 5). Then John hears as it were the voice of a great multitude praising God (vv. 6-9). First, God is praised for he reigns as the Almighty (cf. ESV). Secondly, God is praised for the marriage of the Lamb has come. "Is the church not yet married to Christ? Of course it is (Rom. 7:4; Eph. 5:22ff). There is another sense in which there is a 'final consummation' between Christ and his bride (Alford). This will occur when the Lord ultimately receives the church unto himself at the end of time (21:1ff)."[4]

The bride (the church) prepares herself for her marriage to the Lamb by adorning herself in fine linen (which is the righteous acts of the saints, v. 8) that is clean and bright (showing she has kept herself pure). She does not defile herself by bowing to the influence of Rome. Thus, we see a picture of victory – the pure bride ready for her husband.

John is overwhelmed by the scene and thus falls down to worship the angel. Perhaps Lenski is right when he says, "There is, as far as we can see, only one explanation for his action here as well as in 22:8: he mistakes the speaker for the Lord himself."[5] At any rate, he is rebuked for it and is told to worship God (v. 10; cf. 22:8). The angel presents himself as a fellow servant to John and his brethren in the work of presenting the testimony of Jesus. They are engaged in the same work and are on the same level, thus he is not deserving of worship. The angel explains, "For the testimony of Jesus is the spirit of prophecy." That is, the message of Jesus is the essence of prophecy.[6] The New Living Translation renders this, "For the essence of prophecy is to give a clear witness for Jesus." That was their work and the reason for not worshipping the angel.

Christ the Victorious Warrior (vv. 11-21)

The victory celebrated in the first ten verses is only possible because of Christ who is the victorious warrior. "Up to this point he has been pictured as Lion, Lamb, Judge, and now he is a victorious Warrior."[7]

Christ on a white horse (vv. 11-16). The scene changes and John sees the heavens open and a rider on a white horse. The titles given to him and the description leave no doubt that the rider is the Christ.

There are four titles by which he is called: (vv. 11, 13, 16). He is Faithful and True (v. 11; cf. 1:5; 3:7, 14). He is trustworthy, reliable and worthy of all confidence. He is the Word of God (v. 13; cf. John 1:1; 1 John 1:1, 4). He is the ultimate revelation of the will of God. The message of God is embodied in Christ. He is "God's utterance to man."[8] He is King of kings (v. 16) and Lord of Lords (v. 16). He has supreme rule over all.

His mission is that of a warrior for he judges and makes war (vv. 11, 14-15). His armies follow him (v. 14). Out of his mouth comes a sharp sword by which he strikes the nations (v. 15).

---

4 Wayne Jackson, *Revelation: Jesus Christ's Final Message of Hope – Select Studies from the Apocalypse*, 214.
5 R. C. H. Lenski, *The Interpretation of St. John's Revelation*, 545.
6 Prophecy seems to be used here in the sense of the revelation of God's will more than a reference to Old Testament prophecies of Christ.
7 Summers, *ibid.*, 197.
8 Summers, *ibid.*, 197

The description of the rider is most interesting (vv. 12, 13, 15). His *eyes are like a flame of fire* (v. 12). He "looks with burning penetration into the hearts of His enemies."[9] The fire may come from his wrath that he executes as a warrior. He wears *many crowns* (v. 12). A crown is worn by royalty – one who rules. The many crowns tell us that his rule and power is over all. It may also suggest many victories have been won. His *robe was dipped in blood* (v. 13). The blood, no doubt, is the blood of his enemies (cf. Isa. 63:2-3) from trampling the winepress of the wrath of God (Rev. 14:20). Lastly, he is described as having a *sharp sword coming out of his mouth* (v. 15). The mighty warrior is ready for battle.

The defeat of the beast and his armies (vv. 17-21). The chapter closes with a declaration of victory, even before the battle begins. The battle will not be long. It is soon over. The Christ, who sits on his white horse, is victorious. John sees an angel that cries with a loud voice inviting the birds of the air to eat the carcasses of the armies (vv. 17-18, 21). This is a picture of complete victory. The beast (the sea beast, Rev. 13:1-10) along with the false prophet (the land beast, Rev. 13:11-18) are captured and cast in the lake of fire – doomed to eternal destruction (vv. 19-20). Not only is the beast defeated, but his armies (his allies) are killed (v. 21).

This is the battle of Armageddon that we see in Revelation 16 (lesson 20). As we pointed out there, this is not a literal battle. Armageddon simply stands for a decisive battle between the forces of Satan and the Lamb of God. The battle is fought. The Lamb of God wins in a decisive victory.

"In this chapter of Revelation the familiar military symbolism is pressed to its limit to create the proper impression – certain victory for the cause of righteousness over the beast, the false prophet, and their allies. This meant freedom from persecution for the Christians. The pagan religion and godless government of Rome were doomed to fall. And when they fell, God's cause, God's people, God's purposes go right on living and growing. At such points as this in the book, the philosophy of history school makes its bids for recognition. Their verdict would be: 'This symbolizes the complete victory of the Son of God over all hosts of wickedness, not just in John's age but in any age of the world's history.' That is true, but the primary emphasis is on the victory over the pagan false religion of Asia Minor about A.D. 95."[10]

Questions

1. What three things does the multitude say in praise to God? _____
   _____
   _____

2. When does the marriage of the Lamb and his bride occur? _____
   _____
   _____

3. How does the bride prepare herself for her husband in this text? _____
   _____
   _____

---

9   Homer Hailey, *Revelation, An Introduction and Commentary*, 382.
10 Summer, *ibid.*, 201

4. Why does John attempt to worship an angel? _____
_____

5. What reason does the angel give that John should not worship him? _____
_____

6. Throughout this book, Christ is pictured as the Lion, Lamb, Judge, and now he is a victorious _____.

7. What does the description of eyes like a flame of fire tell us about the Christ? _____
_____
_____

8. What does the description of many crowns tell us about the Christ? _____
_____
_____

9. What does the description of robe dipped in blood tell us about the Christ? _____
_____
_____

10. What is the main point of this chapter? _____
_____
_____

Revelation 20
Lesson 24
Victory Over Satan and The Final Judgment

Outline

I. Victory over Satan (vv. 1-10)

   A. Satan bound for 1,000 years (vv. 1-3)

   B. The reign of martyrs and faithful saints (vv. 4-6)

   C. Satan overthrown forever (vv. 7-10)
   1. Released from prison (v. 7)
   2. Goes out to deceive nations and battle with saints (vv. 8-9a)
   3. Satan devoured and cast into the lake of fire (vv. 9b-10)

II. The Final Judgment (vv. 11-15)

   A. God on the great white throne (v. 11)

   B. Dead stand before God to be judged (vv. 12-13)

   C. Those not in the book of life – cast into the lake of fire (vv. 14-15)

Key Verse that Summarizes the Chapter

Revelation 20:10

The devil, who deceived them, was cast into the lake of fire and brimstone where the beast and the false prophet are. And they will be tormented day and night forever and ever.

The theme of chapters 19-21 is the victory of God's people.[1] Beginning with chapter 12, three enemies of God and his people have worked together in an effort to destroy the Lord's church. The beast and the harlot have worked as tools of Satan. As the previous chapter closed, two of the three enemies are gone. The one enemy (Satan) remains. In this chapter, we see a picture of victory over Satan (vv. 1-10) as well as a scene of the final judgement (vv. 11-15).

There are several difficulties as we work through this chapter. Dan King said it well, "Some of these symbols used in this chapter have been like the proverbial prickly pear cactus, hard to

---

[1] Look back to lesson 1 for an outline of the book of Revelation.

handle and downright painful if mishandled."[2] Summers cautioned the reader saying, "This chapter needs to be approached with great humility of spirit, a recognition of its difficulties, an avoidance of dogmatic statements, and respect for the honest interpretation of others."[3]

Some of the problems with this chapter include questions about the 1,000 years. What is the period of 1000 years? When does it start? And, when is it over? Likewise, the binding of Satan poses some questions. How and when was he bound? When and in what way is he loosed (v. 7)?

In spite of the difficulties (and various interpretations of conservative scholars), the main point of the chapter is clear: victory over Satan. The theme is the defeat of Satan, not the 1,000 year reign. If, when one is through with the chapter, there are still questions about the 1,000 years and the binding of Satan, the main point does not have to be missed.

Victory over Satan (vv. 1-10)

The first ten verses focus on victory over Satan. Again, let us not lose sight of this point.

Satan bound for 1,000 years (vv. 1-3). John sees an angel coming down from heaven with the key to the bottomless pit and a great chain in his hand. The key suggests that he has authority over the bottomless pit including the power to bind one in it. The chain is used to bind. None of these are literal (the key, the pit or the chain), but are symbolic, fitting the nature of the rest of the book. The angel lays hold of Satan, binds him and casts him into the bottomless pit.

There are four terms used to refer to Satan (v. 2). He is called the *dragon* because he is strong and powerful. He is called the *serpent* because he deceives and tempts as he did in the garden (2 Cor. 11:3). He is called the *Devil* because he is the accuser or slanderer. He is called *Satan* because he is our adversary or opponent.

What is the 1000 year period? Any interpretation must have some significance to the recipients of the book of Revelation because it pertains to things that would shortly come to pass (1:1; 22:6).

This is not about a literal 1000 year period wherein Christ reigns on a literal throne in Jerusalem after the second coming as the Premillennialist claim. First, the book is written in symbolic language (1:1). Secondly, if the 1000 years is to be taken literal, then so must the key (v. 1), the bottomless pit (v. 1), the great chain (v. 1), the dragon (v. 2), and the serpent (v. 2). Third, there are several things essential to the premillennial thought that are not found in this chapter: the second coming, a bodily resurrection, the reign of Christ on earth, the Jews return to Palestine, Christ on earth, Jerusalem, and the literal throne of David. This point is clear to the careful student of the text. However, many of us are better at explaining what the 1000 years is not than we are at explaining what it is.

Obviously, the 1000 years is symbolic. "Numbers in Revelation are symbolical. 'Ten' is a complete number, and 'one thousand' is a high multiple of ten. The number is to be understood as an idea of completeness. It does not represent a period of years either before or after the second coming of Christ. It tells John's readers that the devil is going to be completely

---

2   Daniel H. King, Sr., *The Book of Revelation*, 69.
3   Ray Summers, *Worthy is the Lamb*, 202.

restrained from deceiving the nations into worshipping the emperor."[4] Consider how "one thousand" is used throughout the Bible representing something that is full and complete (Deut. 5:10; 7:9; Job 9:3; 33:23; Psa. 50:10; 90:4; 105:8; Ecc. 6:6; 7:28; 2 Pet. 3:8). Thus, the 1000 years is symbolic of a full and complete period that is not specified. It symbolizes the complete victory over Satan.

So when does the 1000 year period occur? It would be when Christ is also reigning (v 4). He reigns from his ascension until the second coming (Dan. 7:13-14; 1 Cor. 15:22-24). If it is the time of victory over Satan when he is no longer deceiving the nations (v. 3), then it begins shortly from the time of the writing of the book. "This leads to the conclusion that the thousand years symbolizes that period of victory beginning with Constantine, when Roman persecution ended, and continuing until some time before the Lord's return when Satan will be loosed from his present restraint."[5]

What is the binding of Satan and when does it occur? When Satan is cast into the bottomless pit (abyss, ASV), it is not for his punishment (that comes later, v. 10), but to prevent and limit his power. This limitation is explained, "so that he should deceive the nations no more till the thousand years were finished" (v. 3). His control is limited. He is bound in the sense that he suffers defeat.[6] The power he had when using Domitian (the beast) and the Roman Empire (the Harlot) as his allies is taken away. There has not been a world empire with the power to persecute like Rome did since.

This does not mean that Satan lost all power and is thus completely inactive. Perhaps Hailey said it best, "The binding of Satan does not render him absolutely helpless or unable to operate; for he continues to be exceedingly active. He walks about as a roaring lion, seeking whom he may devour (1 Peter 5:8); but his activity is limited, as a dog chained to a wire between two trees. He can operate only within the limited distance between the trees, and to the length of the chain from side to side. In this binding, Satan is divinely restrained from reestablishing control over the nations."[7]

After this binding (cast into the bottomless pit) Satan is released for a little while (v. 3). This will be explained at verse 7.

The reign of martyrs and faithful saints (vv. 4-6). While Satan is bound, John sees the souls of those who had suffered for the Lord (cf. 6:9-11) living and reigning with Christ for 1000 years. We have already seen that the 1000 years is not literal or a period of time after the second coming. It is a picture of complete victory of the saints. In chapter six (vv. 9-11) we see the souls under the altar crying out for judgement (a scene of seeming defeat). By contrast, here, we see the souls sitting on thrones given victory. What an encouragement to those whose loved ones had died as martyrs, knowing they now reign with Christ.

Those who apply this passage to a period beyond the second coming fail to note that those in this passage who live and reign with Christ were those who were beheaded (v. 4). Verse 5 pictures the victory of the martyrs as a resurrection. This is not a bodily resurrection, but symbolic of their victory over Satan. In the Old Testament, victory over idolatry

---

[4] Summers, *ibid.*, 204.
[5] Homer Hailey, *Revelation, An Introduction and Commentary*, 392.
[6] Compare Matthew 12:29; Mark 3:27 where the limiting of Satan's power is referred to as binding him.
[7] Homer Hailey, *ibid.*, 391.

and captivity is pictured as a resurrection (Isa. 26:19; Hos. 13:14; Ezek. 37:1-14). These martyrs who experience this first resurrection will not be hurt in the second death (v. 6) which is eternal hell (Rev. 20:14; 21:8).

The "rest of the dead" probably refers to the wicked who died by the sword of Christ in the battle scene of the previous chapter (19:21). They do not live again (a resurrection) until after the 1000 years. Just as the victory of the saints is not a literal bodily resurrection, neither is this. Their cause is revived after the 1000 years (explained at verse 7).

Satan overthrown forever (vv. 7-10). This section pictures a complete overthrow of Satan for eternity. But first, he is released from his prison – the abyss (v. 7). Without a doubt this is a difficult point to grasp, much less explain. "We can only suggest as to where or in what way Satan was loosed."[8]

So in what way is Satan released for a little while (v. 3) from his prison (v. 7)? "Perhaps it signifies a period of great wickedness just before the second coming of Christ, comparable to the days of Noah before the flood (Luke 17:26-27)."[9] One writer suggests it means that Rome is not God's or the church's final enemy.[10] Others will follow.

When Satan is released, he goes out to deceive nations and battle with the saints (vv. 8-9a). Gog and Magog align with Satan to surround the camp of the saints. This is an obvious reference to Ezekiel 38-39 where Gog of the land of Magog symbolizes the enemies of Israel that fight against them, but are defeated by God. It is used here to represent another effort of Satan to fight against God and his people. This is not a physical battle, but a spiritual one.

Even though Satan is loosed and strives to do his damage again, he is devoured and cast into the lake of fire (vv. 9b-10). This section closes with the beast, false prophet and the devil all in the eternal hell.

Whatever the meaning of the loosing of Satan, the main point is the same: he will be defeated. Since more is not told, we evidently don't need to know more than this. "There is a total lack of detail here. Only a summary depiction of a victory brought about by divine rather than human agency and power. This is all God wanted his people to know, namely that in the end he will bring about the downfall of their mutual enemies and give the victory to his faithful people. Evidently that is all they needed to know then and need to know now."[11]

The Final Judgment (vv. 11-15)

Having mentioned the final destiny of Satan (v. 10), the scene now shifts to the final judgment. How does this help the intended readers of the book dealing with the pressures from Rome? It gives assurance and comfort to the faithful as they get a glimpse of the judgment and final victory (chapter 21).

---

8   Homer Hailey, *ibid.*, 396.
9   Robert Harkrider, *Revelation*, 231.
10 Daniel H. King, Sr., *ibid.*, 71.
11 Daniel H. King., Sr., *ibid.*, 71.

God on the great white throne (v. 11). John sees a great white throne with God[12] sitting on the throne. Earth and heaven fled away in the sense that they will be no more (2 Pet. 3:10). From this throne judgment is executed.

Dead stand before God to be judged (vv. 12-13). John sees the dead, small and great, (all mankind) standing before the throne to be judged. The books that are opened are probably the record of the deeds (works, v. 12) of those to be judged.[13] Another book is opened which is the Book of Life, which is the register of the names of the righteous (cf. Exo. 32:32-33; Psa. 69:27-28; Mal. 3:16-17; Luke 10:20; Phil. 4:13; Rev. 3:5; 21:27).

The sea which gave up the dead, is probably used in the same sense it was in chapter 13 referring to the mass of humanity (v. 13). The point is that all will be judged.

Those not in the book of life – cast into the lake of fire (vv. 14-15). Death and Hades are cast into the lake of fire for at the judgment both are brought to an end. The lake of fire (eternal hell) is the second death. Anyone, whose name is not in the book of life, is cast into the lake of fire.

So, what is the main point of the chapter? It is victory over Satan.

Questions

1. The theme is the _____ _____ _____, not the _____ _____ _____.

2. Four terms are used in this chapter to refer to Satan. What are they and what do they mean?
   a. _____ Meaning: _____
   b. _____ Meaning: _____
   c. _____ Meaning: _____
   d. _____ Meaning: _____

3. List some things in the context of Revelation 20 that must be taken literal if we interpret the 1,000 years as literal. _____

4. List some things that are essential points of premillennialism that are not found in Revelation 20. _____

---

12 This may have reference to Christ, rather than the Father, since all judgment is given to the Son (John 5:22).
13 Some suggest that the books (plural) may be the standard (law) by which the people will be judged. Those from different dispensations will be judged by the laws under which they lived.

5. If the 1,000 years are symbolic, what do they represent? _____

6. When does the 1,000 years occur? _____

7. In what way is Satan bound? _____

8. What is the second death? _____

9. How would a look at the judgment scene (vv. 11-15) help the intended readers of the book dealing with the pressures from Rome? _____

10. Who or what is Gog and Magog? _____

Revelation 21

Lesson 25
Victory in Heaven

Outline

I. Perfect Fellowship with God (vv. 1-8)

    A. *God's people who overcome will be with God (vv. 1-7)*
        1. New heaven and new earth (new order) (v. 1)
        2. No more sea (v. 1)
        3. New Jerusalem – as bride adorned for her husband (v. 2).
        4. God dwells with this people (v. 3)
        5. Former things are passed away – all things become new (vv. 4-5)
        6. Drink of water of life freely (v. 6)
        7. Inheritance as God's children (v. 7)

    B. *Those who are not God's people will not be there (v. 8)*
        1. The cowardly, unbelievers, abominable, murderers, sexually immoral, sorcerers, idolaters and all liars
        2. In a lake of fire

II. The New Jerusalem (vv. 9-27)

    A. *Angel showed John the great city (vv. 9-11)*

    B. *Exterior of the city (vv. 12-21)*
        1. Great and high wall (v. 12)
        2. Twelve gates (vv. 12-13)
        3. Twelve foundations (v. 14)
        4. Measurement of the city (vv. 15-17)
        5. Materials used – glory of the city (vv. 18-21)

    C. *Interior of the city (vv. 22-27)*
        1. God and Lamb are the temple (v. 22)
        2. Glory of God is the light (v.23)
        3. Gates are not shut at all (v. 25)
        4. No night there (v. 25)
        5. Those in the city (vv. 24, 27)
            a. Saved walk in it (v. 24)
            b. The glory of the nations (vv. 24, 26)
            c. Those whose names are in the book of life (v. 27)
            d. Nothing that defiles will enter in (v. 27)

> **Key Verse that Summarizes the Chapter**
>
> **Revelation 21:1**
>
> Now I saw a new heaven and a new earth, for the first heaven and the first earth had passed away. Also there was no more sea.

This, along with the previous two chapters, deals with the victory of God's people.[1] The beast, the harlot and Satan have been defeated. John is also given a view of the final judgment (20:11-15). Here, the picture is the ultimate victory in heaven.

There are two different views of this chapter. One says it is a picture of God's people in heaven, while the other says it is a view of the church on earth in a post persecution period. The evidence is abundant that this is a picture of heaven. (1) This follows the final judgment scene in the previous chapter (20:11-15). (2) God is seen (22:4)[2], which could not be true in the church on earth. (3) The throne of God is there (22:3) which is in heaven (Psa. 89:29). (4) The picture of verses 1-7 is put in contrast to eternal hell (21:8). (5) The new heavens and earth (v. 1) is used in 2 Peter 3:13 to refer to heaven. (6) There is no more death (21:4). If the passage refers to heaven, the application is obvious. However, if it is a picture of the church on earth, is this physical death or spiritual death? (7) Those present will reign forever and ever (22:5). (8) Those who enter do so after their name is written in the book of life (21:27). (9) We must consider the value this has to the first readers of the book. They were already in the church. This chapter would be a look at the future when things would be totally different (i.e. 21:4).

In this chapter (and the first five verses of the next), heaven is presented from three viewpoints: (1) a tabernacle wherein there is perfect fellowship with God (21:1-8), (2). a city wherein there is perfect protection by God (21:9-27), and (3) a garden wherein there is perfect provision by God (22:1-5).[3]

Perfect Fellowship with God (vv. 1-8)

God's people who overcome will be with God (vv. 1-7). The assurances of theses verses are given to those who overcome (v. 7). They will be allowed to dwell with God in perfect fellowship.

First John sees a new heaven and new earth (v. 1). This language is borrowed from Isaiah 65:17 (cf. 66:22) which foretold of the days of the Messiah. When the Christ came, there was not a literal new heaven and literal new earth, but simply a new order in contrast to the old (under the Old Testament era). So here in our text, the future in heaven is pictured as a new order in contrast to life here on earth. Peter makes the same use of the expression (2 Pet. 3:13).

---

1 Look back to lesson 1 for an outline of the book of Revelation.
2 Whatever the scene is in chapter 21, it continues into chapter 22.
3 Taken from Ray Summers, *Worthy is the Lamb*, 212-214.

In the new order there is no more sea (v. 1). At the throne scene (4:6), the sea prevented access to the throne. In John's vision of the future, the obstacle is now removed.[4]

John describes what he saw as a holy city, a New Jerusalem, prepared as a bride adorned for her husband (v. 2). "The purpose here is, to represent it as exceedingly beautiful."[5] The idea of purity may also be suggested being that those within have overcome (v. 7). A voice from heaven explained to John what he saw, "Behold, the tabernacle of God *is* with men, and He will dwell with them, and they shall be His people. God Himself will be with them *and be* their God" (v. 3). "Tabernacle" means to dwell. The ESV renders this verse, "Behold, the dwelling place of God is with man." "So the New Jerusalem is a tabernacle where God dwells with his people."[6] God has dwelt with his people in the tabernacle, the temple and the church. Now, in John's vision the dwelling of God with his people has reached perfection – dwelling with his people forever.

In this blessed state the very things the suffering Christians (to whom this book is addressed) experienced will have passed away (v. 4). There will be no tears, death, sorrow, crying or pain. God promises to make all things new (v. 5). As a guarantee that the reader can depend on this being true, John is told to write (v. 5).

The one on the throne said, "It is done" (v. 6). "The meaning in the passage before us evidently is, 'The great work is accomplished; the arrangement of human affairs is complete. The redeemed are gathered in; the wicked are cut off; truth is triumphant, and all is now complete—prepared for the eternal state of things.'"[7] Such an affirmation could only be made by one who is the Alpha and Omega, the Beginning and the End.

The picture being drawn of heaven is one having continual access to the fountain of the water of life (v. 6), and receiving an inheritance as a son (v. 7).

Those who are not God's people will not be there (v. 8). "But" shows a contrast. Those who are not God's faithful will not be in heaven as described in verses 1-7. This includes the cowardly (fearful, ASV- those who are afraid to stand and do what is right), the unbelieving (faithless, ESV - those who do not have sincere faith), abominable (detestable, ESV – those who are disgusting because of their sins), murderers, sexually immoral, sorcerers (those who practice magical arts and witchcraft), idolaters, and all liars. These will have their part in the lake that burns with fire and brimstone.[8] Eternal hell is here called the second death (cf. 2:11; 20:6, 14).

The New Jerusalem (vv. 9-27)

As noted earlier, this section looks at a city wherein there is perfect protection by God. Earlier (v. 2) John saw the holy city, the New Jerusalem, coming down out of heaven. This section (vv. 9-27) is not another vision, but details about what he saw in this city.

---

4 Others interpret the "no more sea" to refer to the sea from which the beast arose (chapter 13). There the sea referred to the mass of humanity. If this is the sea referred to in chapter 21, the point would be there is no more sea (society) from which a beast like Domitian could arise.
5 Albert Barnes, *Notes on the New Testament: Revelation*, 444.
6 Summers, *ibid.*, 212.
7 Barnes, *ibid.*, 445.
8 The NIV translates this "fiery lake of burning sulfur."

Angel showed John the great city (vv. 9-11). One of the seven angels that had the seven bowls of wrath (Rev. 15) called John to come and see the Lamb's bride (the church, Eph. 5). John was taken in a vision to a high mountain where he saw the great city, the holy Jerusalem (v.10). He was not shown something different than he was told. Rather, he saw the Lamb's bride (the church) in its final home in the holy city. No greater description of its splendor can be given than its "having the glory of God" (v. 11).

Exterior of the city (vv. 12-21). John proceeds to describe the exterior of the city. Keep in mind that this is not a literal city. The terms used here (wall, gates, and foundation) are not literal, but symbolic, harmonizing with the rest of the book.

The city had a great and high wall (v. 12) which symbolizes complete and perfect protection. The wall had twelve gates (vv. 12-13). The number twelve is the religious number (12 tribes, 12 apostles, etc.). The names of the twelve tribes were written on the gates which may suggest that all of God's people (from both the Old and New Testament periods) will abide in the city. The twelve angels at the gates may symbolize the protection provided within the walls of the city.

There were twelve foundations supporting the city (v. 14). Summers observed "...so perfect a foundation could not be shaken."[9] The names of the twelve apostles were on the twelve foundations. "These dual 'twelves' perhaps suggest the presence of God's faithful from both the Old and New Testament eras."[10]

The measurement of the city (vv. 15-17) is not to be taken literal. The point is to emphasize its glory. The length, breadth and height measured 12,000 furlongs. "To make this into a literal number destroys the symbolism. Twelve thousand furlongs is equivalent to 1,500 miles in present-day measurements, but that has no meaning."[11] Twelve thousand is a multiple of twelve (the religious number). Thus, this is a full and complete number. There is ample room for all of God's people. The wall measured 144 cubits. Again, the number twelve multiplied by itself may suggest absolute and complete protection for those within – the people of God.

The materials used reflect the glory of the city (vv. 18-21). The wall was made of jasper (probably diamond, v. 18). The city was pure gold, like clear glass (v. 18). The foundations had twelve different precious stones. Some of these are hard to identify with certainty. However, the point is still gained – we see the glory and magnificence of the city.

Interior of the city (vv. 22-27). John turns to describe what he saw within the city. There is no temple, for God and the Lamb are the temple (v. 22). The temple is where God met his people. There is no need for a temple for God and the Lamb dwell with their people. There is no need of the sun or moon for God's glory illuminates the city (v. 23). There is no need to shut the gates (as cities of old would do) for there is no night there (v. 25).

The last thing John does in the chapter is focus on those in the city (vv. 24, 26, 27). The saved walk within the city (v. 24). The glory and honor of the nations will be brought into the city (vv. 24, 26). "The City of God will have the best of all the nations (Is. 60:5, 11)..."[12] The Gentiles are included. Only those whose names are in the Lamb's book of life are allowed

---

9   *ibid.*, 213.
10   Wayne Jackson, *Revelation, Jesus Christ's Final Message of Hope*, 221.
11   Summers, *ibid.*,213.
12   A. T. Robertson, *Word Pictures in the New Testament* (Rev. 21:26).

in the city (v. 27). Nothing that defiles, causes an abomination or a lie will enter in (v. 27). This is ultimate security, perfect protection, and absolute safety.

So, what is the main point of this chapter? The ultimate victory of God's people in heaven.

Questions

1. Does this chapter describe heaven or the church in a post-persecution period? _____

2. Heaven is presented from what three viewpoints in this chapter and the first five verses of the next chapter? _____

3. What does "new heaven and new earth" mean? _____

4. What is the significance of "no more sea" (v. 1)? _____

5. What is meant by "the tabernacle of God is with men" (v. 3)? _____

6. What is being affirmed in "it is done" (v. 6)? _____

7. The angel told John he was going to show him the Lamb's bride, but he showed him the holy city, Jerusalem. Did he show him something different? If not, how is this explained? _____

8. Why is there no need for a temple in the new Jerusalem? _____

9. Who will be in the holy city—the new Jerusalem (vv. 24-27)? _____

10. What is the main point of this chapter? _____

Revelation 22

Lesson 26
Warnings About the Book

Outline

IV. Life in the New Jerusalem (vv. 1-5)

   A. *River of water proceeds from the throne (v. 1)*

   B. *Tree of life (v. 2)*
     1. In middle of street on either side of river
     2. Twelve fruits
     3. Leaves are for healing of the nations

   C. *Dwell with God (vv. 3-5)*
     1. No curse (v. 3)
     2. Serve God (v. 3)
     3. See his face (v. 4)
     4. His name written on their foreheads (v. 4)
     5. No night there and no need of light – God gives the light (v. 5)
     6. Reign forever and ever (v. 5)

V. Warnings (vv. 6-21)

   A. *Time is near (vv. 6-11)*
     1. Must shortly take place (v. 6)
     2. Coming quickly (v. 7)
     3. Time is at hand (v. 10)
     4. Period of probation has ended (v. 11)

   B. *Heed the message (vv. 7, 12-17)*
     1. Blessed if keep words of this book (v. 7)
     2. God will give to everyone according to works (v. 12)
     3. Must keep commandments to enter into city of heaven (vv. 14-15)
     4. Invitation to come and drink of water of life (vv. 16-17)

   C. *Do not add to or take away (vv. 18-19)*

   D. *The Lord comes quickly (v. 20)*

> **Key Verses that Summarize the Chapter**
> **Revelation 22:18-19**
>
> ¹⁸For I testify to everyone who hears the words of the prophecy of this book: If anyone adds to these things, God will add to him the plagues that are written in this book;
> ¹⁹and if anyone takes away from the words of the book of this prophecy, God shall take away his part from the Book of Life, from the holy city, and from the things which are written in this book.

This chapter begins with the third of three viewpoints of heaven.[1] In the previous chapter, we saw (1) a tabernacle wherein there is perfect fellowship with God (21:1-8), and (2) a city wherein there is perfect protection by God (21:9-27). This chapter presents (3) a garden wherein there is perfect provision by God (22:1-5).

Life in the New Jerusalem (vv. 1-5)

Even a casual reading of these verses reminds us of the Garden of Eden which has the tree of life (Gen. 2:9) and a river in its midst (v. 10). When man sinned (Gen. 3:1-6), a curse was pronounced upon man and the earth (vv. 14-24). In the verses before us, we see that which was lost in Eden will be gained in heaven.

River of water proceeds from the throne (v. 1). John was shown a river of water of life flowing from the throne of God and the Lamb.[2] The water that sustains life comes from the throne of God (thus God himself).

Tree of life (v. 2). On each side of the river was the tree of life. Hailey helps clear some of the difficulty in the wording of the text, "The picture is difficult to visualize but it seems that in the midst of the streets, viewed collectively as one, the river flows alongside with trees on its banks. The tree of life, singular, 'on this side of the river and on that,' indicates that 'tree' is used collectively, as is 'street,' to represent all the trees that lined the river."[3]

If one eats from the tree of life (Rev. 2:7; 22:14) he will live forever (Gen. 3:22). Rather than an annual fruit, each tree bore its fruit every month. The tree perpetually bears. Thus, an abundance of fruit. The leaves of the tree have healing (spiritual) powers. Man's basic needs (water, food and health) are completely supplied. Obviously, this is all symbolic pointing to the perfect provision of eternal life.

Dwell with God (vv. 3-5). These verses describe the perfect condition of dwelling with God in the new Jerusalem. There is no more curse (v. 3).[4] "The curse imposed in Eden is now removed, implying, for one thing, that death will be no more (cf. 21:4)."[5] The faithful servants of God serve him throughout eternity (v. 3). They see God's face (v. 4). The desire of man to

---

1 Taken from Ray Summers, *Worthy is the Lamb*, 212-214.
2 We are reminded of Ezekiel 47:1-12 where Ezekiel sees a vision of a river flowing from the temple. See also Joel 3:18 and Zechariah 14:8.
3 Homer Hailey, *Revelation, An Introduction and Commentary*, 422.
4 Compare Revelation 21:27.
5 Wayne Jackson, *Revelation, Jesus Christ's Final Message of Hope*, 223.

see God (John 14:8) is not realized until eternity (cf. 1 John 3:2). What a scene of standing before God with his name on your forehead showing you are one of his own. There is no need for a lamp or the sun for God gives the light for all in the new Jerusalem (v. 5). In this perfect condition of dwelling with God, the saints reign for all eternity.

This marks the end of John's vision. What remains are four warnings about the book that are designed to impress upon the reader the importance of the message.

Warnings (vv. 6-21)

Time is near (vv. 6-11). First, God puts his stamp of approval upon the Revelation by having his angel tell John, "These words are faithful and true" (v. 6).[6] The message of the book is about things "which must shortly take place" (v. 6; 1:1).[7] The events described in the book are not a prophecy of what would develop hundreds or thousands of years later. Rather, this gives the assurance of immediate or near fulfillment of the promise of victory.

The Lord promises to come quickly (v. 7, 12, 20). This is not the second coming, for it is not at hand (2 Thess. 2:1-ff). Rather, it is a coming in judgment (in time) upon Rome. Because the events are to shortly take place, a blessing is held out to those who keep the words of this book (v. 7).

When John hears these things, he falls down before the angel to worship him and is quickly corrected (vv. 8-9). Why he does this we are not told. He has made the same mistake once before (19:10). Does he mistake the angel for the Lord (the Christ)? Or is he so relieved to hear that the time is near that he feels the messenger is worthy of praise? At any rate, the angel turns from John's mistake back to the message of the time being near (v. 10). He instructs John not to seal the words of the prophecy of this book because the "time is at hand" (v. 10). The events described would take place in the near future. Notice that the message of the book is sandwiched between statements at the beginning and end of the book that these things must shortly take place (1:1; 22:6) and the time is at hand (1:3; 22:10).

Since the time is near, the period of probation has ended (v. 11). Those who are the enemies of God's people continue in their ungodliness in spite of any warnings. Those who are the faithful of God are encouraged to press on in their righteousness and holiness.

Heed the message (vv. 7, 12-17). The second warning is to take heed to the message. We have already noticed a blessing pronounced upon one who keeps the words of this book (v. 7). The Lord coming quickly (v. 12) is the same as in verse 7 and in context with "things which must shortly take place" (v. 6) and "the time is at hand" (v. 10). It does not refer to the Lord's second coming, for it was not at hand (2 Thess. 2). Rather, it is a coming in judgment (in time). The Lord promises to reward everyone according to his work (v. 12). This may refer to a reward when the Lord judges (in time), but the principle obviously applies to the Lord's final coming. Certainly, this verse gives assurance to those resisting the pressures of Rome that the Lord is coming quickly in judgment on Rome, but his reward[8] (to the good

---

6   Jesus, the Son, gives his stamp of approval (v. 16), as well as John giving his testimony of what he heard (v. 8). At least three witnesses (four counting the angel, v. 6) testify to the truthfulness of the book.
7   The time is at hand (v. 10).
8   ESV: "Behold, I am coming soon, bringing my recompense with me, to repay each one for what he has done" (v. 12)

and evil) not only affects their present outlook (victory over their enemy), but includes the hope of heaven (cf. v. 14).

The one who makes this promise of coming and bringing the reward (the Christ) calls himself the Alpha and the Omega, the First and the Last, the Beginning and the End (v. 12). This affirms his eternal nature, and thus his deity.

Only those who do the commandments of God enter the heavenly city and partake of the tree of life (v. 14). Outside of the city are those who are cast into the lake of fire (cf. 21:8). The "dogs" are those who are morally impure, including homosexuals (cf. Deut. 23:17-18; Phil. 3:2). The rest of the list in verse 15 is repeated from Revelation 21:8.

This third warning closes with an invitation to come and drink of the water of life (vv. 16-17). Jesus, along with the Father (v. 6), puts his stamp of approval on the message of the book (v. 16). He is both the root (the source) and the offspring (descendant) of David (v. 16). That very point had baffled the Jews (Matt. 22:42-46). This again affirms his deity. He is the bright and morning star that gives hope and promise for the future. "And as the morning star, He heralds the approach of eternal day."[9] Along with the Christ, the Spirit and the bride (the church) say, "Come" and partake of the water of life (v. 17).[10]

Do not add to or take away (vv. 18-19). The third warning is not to add to or take away from the message of this book. This book is true, for God (v. 6) and Christ (v. 16), along with John (v. 8) have testified to it being from God. Thus, man is not to change the divine message. These verses are talking about the message of this book, but the principle applies to the rest of the revealed word of God (Deut. 4:2).

The Lord comes quickly (v. 20). The fourth and final warning closes the book with the promise of the Lord saying "Surely I am coming quickly." This must have reference to the same "coming" as in verses 7 and 12. He is coming quickly in judgment (in time) on Rome.[11] John adds a plea, "Even so, come, Lord Jesus!" While we may (and can, in fact, should) make that plea today for the Lord to come, from John's vantage point he was crying out for the Lord to come in the Judgment that is pictured throughout the book and promised in this chapter.

The book ends by saying, "The grace of our Lord Jesus Christ be with you all. Amen" (v. 21). By the grace of God, his people are saved, preserved, and defended against the onslaught of Satan and his allies. It is by the grace of God that the victory in this book will be gained. Amen. So be it.

---

9   Hailey, ibid., 431
10 Some contend, as Hailey does, that the invitation of the Spirit and bride is to the Lord (who promised to come) pleading for him to come. This writer thinks that the verse in question (v. 17) points to an invitation to come to the water of life.
11 If this is referring to the second coming, how would it be "quickly" from the day in which John wrote?

Questions

1. What relation is there between this chapter and the Garden of Eden (in Genesis)? ___

2. What is the tree of life? ___

3. What is meant by "no more curse" (v. 3)? ___

4. What are the four warnings given in this chapter? ___

5. What is the point of this chapter? ___

6. In what sense is the time at hand or near (v. 10)? ___

7. In what sense is the Lord coming quickly (vv. 7, 12, 20)? ___

8. Explain verse 11. ___

9. For class discussion: Why should we ever plea or pray "Even so, come, Lord Jesus"? ___

10. What has impressed you most in this study of the Revelation? ___

www.ingramcontent.com/pod-product-compliance
Lightning Source LLC
LaVergne TN
LVHW061332060426
835512LV00013B/2612